Expecting Revival

Releasing the Power

of

Revival

Through

T.E.A.M. Ministry

R.E. Clark

GnG Publishers
122 Skinner St.
Centerton, AR 72719

Revised and Updated Edition
Published by GnG Publishers
3/21/2014

Original work © 1993 by R.E. Clark released under the title: The T.E.A.M. Concept of Revival Preparation

Printed in the United State of America
Cover photo and some interior photos courtesy: StockPhotosforFree.com

ISBN-13: 978-0615989082
ISBN-10: 061598908X

DEDICATION

When this book was originally released back in 1993 it was dedicated to my wife, Kay, and to the members of Livingston First Baptist Church, who made the T.E.A.M. Concept come alive. I do not think that a dedication should ever be taken back, since those who played an integral part in the first work are still providing that influence. It seems that it would be like unchristening a ship after it has set sail!

As I updated this book, I had to consider many things that have transpired since that original release. Kay is now experiencing the full joy of revival in the presence of her Lord and Savior while the rest of us are awaiting the outpouring of revival rain in our lives and in our churches. God has graciously given me a new companion in my life who walks alongside me in ministry.

Thank you Trudy for your constant encouragement not only in my writing ventures, but in all of my work for the Kingdom of God.

This book is also dedicated to the wonderful churches who are part of the Northwest Arkansas Baptist Association. The folks who are the body of believers in these churches have shown me grace and love as I have served among them for these last 15 years!

Thanks to all of you—past, present. and future!

Table of Contents

INTRODUCTION

It is time for revival in our land.

We need revival in our individual lives, families, and churches. We are at an important juncture in the history of America. We must choose the right way or possibly lose all that we have known for so long. This country was founded on the principles of God's Word and revival played an integral part in her rich history. If we are to see the America that our forefathers knew so well, we must prepare for revival in the land.

The churches of our day are similar to those of England in 1844. Attendance was either dropping or at a plateau and it was again time for the re-invigorating power of revival.[1]

It is my heart's desire to experience a God-sent, Holy Spirit-filled revival. Most pastors and their churches are hoping for the same. The task of writing this book has come from this common consensus. We must find a definitive answer for the frustration of revival efforts in our day.

This book will guide you toward revival. You should know that it is a busy road that leads there. Be in no hurry, for God will have you arrive only when He is ready to revive His people again.

Our churches must begin to believe that revival is possible in our day. No church can experience revival until that body of believers understands their need for revival. Only then can they experience the renewing power of revival blessings.

Revival is not a spectator option, but a participatory obligation. The church needs a new desire for God's presence. We must be willing to pay the price for revival through earnest prayer. This prayer is always based upon the faithfulness of God to provide all according to His divine will.

A change must come to the church for revival to break forth. The church must right herself and like Hezekiah set her house in order (Isaiah 38). The world has crept into the church and we live in a generation that is looking for the parameters of yesteryear. The leadership of the church must be willing to draw clear lines once again for the believer to follow back to God.

When revival occurs, action always follows. A paradox develops here. We must work to see revival, but the real work will not begin until revival comes.

The difference might be summed up in sheer numbers. Normally, only a few will join in the work of revival preparation, but the results will be a reinvigorated work force.

A look into the biblical basis of revival is included in this study. An understanding of God's word, as it speaks of revival, is mandatory to our asking and preparation for revival. Since the focus of this writing is toward preparation for revival, this text will not attempt an in-depth examination of all references to revival. Scriptures will be considered that develop the concept of the need for revival and the preparation for revival.

History provides a rich resource of material to consider in the study of revival. Even though this book is not meant to be an exhaustive historical record, I will provide several references that give us testimony of God's working in the past as He swept people, churches, and lands with the power of His revival winds. The foundation for our present revival work is built upon the stones of previous generations. Historical precedence serves as a record for much that happens in the "mechanics" of the revival meeting.

This study will include the conditions prevalent at the time of these revivals. The results of revival and the personalities of these revivals also will be brought into focus. Much is gained by seeing how God used these men to sweep revival blessings across the land.

These men lived and breathed revival. Henry Ward Beecher said, "Every man must be a revival man."[2] D.M. Panton defined revival as "the inrush of the Spirit into the body that threatens to become a corpse."[3]

As we find ourselves entering a new century, we must consider our methodology of revival. A center must be re-established which considers the time in which we live without forsaking the principles of the Bible. The church has no time to prepare for the rapid changes which we are seeing unfold everyday—but prepare we must.

Most revival literature leaves the reader with many facts, but little by way of direction. The chapters on a plan for revival will be helpful. This plan was used extensively in my ministry and it has proven to be very successful. The plan is geared with the small to medium size church in mind, but it will work in any size church or in any church setting.

Revival should be built around a T.E.A.M. concept. All of the revival planning sections will refer to the T.E.A.M.'s that will be developed. This acronym stands for **Totally Excited About Ministry**. This should be the goal of revival preparation. Revival should equip the saints for the opportunity of ministry which will follow the meetings.

I have incorporated into the chapter on revival planning samples of tools I have used over the years. These are placed in graphical form, so you will be able to see more easily how to use them. From these, you will be able to adapt revival tools for your ministry or local church.

Revival has played an extensive role in history. America has been affected by the winds of revival from her birth. My prayer is that this book will be one small part of a revival sweeping through our nation again.

We have only two options...revival or rapture. Until the rapture, let's have a revival!

CHAPTER ONE

REVIVAL AND THE CHURCH

Someone once asked British evangelist Gypsy Smith how to start a revival. He said, "Lock yourself in your room. Then kneel in the middle of the floor. Draw a chalk mark around yourself and ask God to start a revival inside that chalk mark. When he answers your prayer, the revival will be on."

The church cannot expect revival to begin anywhere but inside her own four walls. The essence of revival dictates that it only comes to the saints of God. Also, it will only come to those who are prepared to receive it in all of its glorious splendor.

Paul wrote concerning a church that is ready for revival, "...that He might present her to Himself a glorious church, not having spot or wrinkle or any such thing, but that she should be holy and without blemish..." (Ephesians 5:27)

Revival is Possible

Some churches have developed a gloom-and-doom philosophy concerning revival. The church and its leadership have effectively given up on revival and the hope of seeing revival in our day.

These views are contrary to the evidence that will be uncovered as we consider the history of revival and its effects upon the church. When all hopes appear smashed, then God reveals Himself as the provider of revival blessing. When men are ready to meet the requirements and standards that God has given, then revival is possible. We must wait upon the Lord "until the Spirit is poured upon us from on high, and the wilderness becomes a fruitful field, and the fruitful field is counted as a forest." (Isaiah 32:15)

Born-Again Believers Only

One of the major concerns in the church today is the problem of the unconverted member. Those who have never had a personal experience with Christ as Savior cannot take part in the blessings of revival.

The revivalists of past centuries were concerned with the reality of unsaved church members. James McGready believed that a man must experience the new birth. This regeneration, which imprints the image of God upon one's soul was of the utmost importance to him and others like him.

McGready stated, "In that awful day, when the universe, assembled, must appear before the quick and dead, the question brethren, will not be, were you a Presbyterian—a Seceder—a Covenantor—a Baptist—or a Methodist; but did you experience a new birth? Did you accept of Christ and his salvation as set forth in the gospel?"[4]

The revival meetings of the First Great Awakening stressed religious experience and results more than correctness of belief, creedal statements, or traditional forms.[5] John Rowland preached for six months during this period of revival. His messages centered upon the subjects of conviction and conversion.

In the three congregations where he preached, the one topic of conversation was "heart religion." Everyone was asking himself whether he was really converted. With this revelation, the convicting power of God came upon entire communities where these churches resided.[6]

Today's preachers and evangelists could take a lesson from these early revivalists. Their primary concern was making sure that the members of those churches in which they preached had a personal relationship with Christ.

It is interesting today that many of what we call revival meetings only cater to the external side of men. Our efforts in revival will not be complete, until men are brought to the point of decision for Christ, and thereby these men are born again.

The Church Needs Revival

Is there a point in time that the church needs revival? We might determine this, if we could only identify a certain age or a single circumstance to mark the time for revival. It is not this simple.

Charles Finney, the revivalist of the nineteenth century, listed several conditions that point to the need for revival.[7] Most of these are prevalent in the church today and most can only be "fixed" with a touch of revival power.

Finney said that revival is needed when there is a lack of brotherly love and Christian confidence among believers. Christians are sometimes noted for boasting about their love for God, but they cannot abide with each other in the local assembly. We are the only group of "soldiers" who quickly bury our wounded with no word of eulogy or comfort.

With the rampant decline in morality now affecting the pulpit, one can understand the lack of confidence among Christians. The only cure for a weakened standard of morality is a revival.

Dissensions, jealousies, and evil rumors were enumerated by Finney as well. More is known today of the local church's last business meeting than of their mission efforts. The tongue is unruly (James 3:1-12) and revival is the only answer for its lack of control.

The church is being affected by a worldly spirit. Finney said that the church had conformed to the world in dress, parties, seeking worldly amusement, and reading filthy novels. He could add a few more to this list of conformities today.

At one time, the church was the uncompromising champion in the war against sin. Now we find the church, as did Finney, "falling into gross and scandalous sins." Revival at the earliest date is necessary to stem the tide of ever increasing depravity.

Finney accused the church of sleeping in his day. He might have chosen a stronger word if he had visited the 21st century. From most observations the word comatose would better describe our condition if he were to accuse us today.

Isaiah wrote that we are much like lazy dogs. "His watchmen are blind, they are all ignorant; they are all dumb dogs, they cannot bark; sleeping, lying down, loving to slumber." (Isaiah 56:10). Finney went on to say, "The fact is, Christians are more to blame for not being revived than sinners are for not being converted."

The church needs revival. Without it, more people from its rolls will die in a year than are added to the church. No one has to be a mathematician to figure the results of this progress. The testimony of this occurrence is seen in the almost empty churches and in those buildings now converted to dance halls, flea markets, etc.

When we forget how to pray, we can be sure that revival is needed. Prayer is the way to revival and revival is the way to prayer.

This is not a continuous loop, with no end in sight. It is the principle of all God's movements in human affairs.[8] George Whitefield said of revival preparation, "Whole days and weeks have I spent prostrate on the ground in silent or vocal prayer."

Revival is intimately connected to the living. It has no place among the spiritually dead. One must have lived if he is to "relive." Much of our revival effort is expended on a church that is primarily dead to spiritual understanding. Should we wonder when our efforts fail and our zeal for revival wanes over time? Unless we experience revival from time to time, the human heart gets crusted over and loses its desire for the divine.[9]

The modem church holds no monopoly on deadness nor have they cornered the market on worldliness. Previous generations were marked by a lack of revival's presence and the effect such a movement had on both the church and the world. The church, both then and now, in this un-revived state lost its influence on the society around them.

More than one hundred years ago England's John Campbell complained to Charles Finney that a general deadness prevailed over the land.[10] These men could have been conversing about the church in the present time.

This deadness is reason enough for revival, but the deadness will not be removed unless the people and the preachers alike seek the freshness of revival rain. Hosea spoke of the condition of the people and he laid the blame at the feet of the priest (Hosea 4:9).

The revivalists of the First Great Awakening told congregations of their deplorable spiritual condition, but they also remarked that the fault was not all their own. The reason they had lost touch with God and could not understand even the principles of salvation was because of poor spiritual guidance by their regular pastors.

Whitefield said, "The generality of preachers talk of an unknown, unfelt Christ. The reason why congregations have been so dead is because they had dead men preaching to them."[11]

Some may disagree that the church today is in such a state. A look at conditions prevalent in the early eighteenth century holds for us a mirror of our church environment today. A glance into the past will reveal much of where we are going in the future.

After the Puritan awakening of the seventeenth century, the church fell into a formalized and routine existence. Church membership became open to many who had no conversion experience and it became difficult to tell the saints from the reprobates. Since there were so few that demonstrated salvation at work in their lives, the majority felt they were no worse than the next. Some ministers baptized all children of respectable parents, though there had been no commitment to Christ.

Times were prosperous and attentions were directed toward making profits and gains. Material success became the watchword for God's blessing. The more goods or the higher the position, the more a person was seen in the eyes of his neighbor as right with God.

A works oriented salvation began to develop. Cotton Mather even urged his congregation to do good to the poor to demonstrate one's concern as a worthy servant of God.

Society began to show the strain of a church in need of revival. Business people cut corners to compete in the markets and farmers charged high prices to cover debts. Political leaders distorted the truth, while town fathers robbed the community treasuries. Lawyers and judges were unable to reach verdicts of justice and special interests groups wielded formidable influence.[12]

We must agree that the conditions of the early eighteenth century are very similar to those of today. The good news is that these conditions, or those like them, often precede outpourings of revival blessing from heaven.

The church needs revival, but she may not quite be aware of it yet. Only as conditions worsen, will hope abound that God will move on the scene. We must come to the place where we can do nothing of our own accord. Only when we have played our last card, and we have nothing left up our proverbial sleeve will we be ready for revival.

The Psalmist cried out in Psalm 85:6, "Will You not revive us again, that Your people may rejoice in You?"

We must be discontent with conditions as they are. Anything but the fresh breeze and life-giving rains of heaven, should leave us dissatisfied. The words of Drury Lacy, a teacher minister at Hampden-Sydney College in Prince Edward County, Virginia, state this idea very well. One September day in 1793, Drury wrote these words to a former student:

> *The dry fields and languishing vines exhibit a too striking picture of the present state of the church. Refreshing showers and fruitful seasons have been restrained, both in the fields and in the assemblies. We but seldom have the pleasure to see persons deeply affected, and tears streaming from their eyes. The harvest seems to be past. God has called his laborers out of this part of his vineyard, and I am left here like an old servant upon a desolate farm. I go around once in a while to keep up the fences; and in good weather; I try to thresh a little. But I have so many complaints, and lazy to boot, that very little is done.*[13]

This minister's heart cry and discontent over the present conditions helped plant the seeds for the Great Revival of the late 1700's. The lack of revival, though disheartening, is not in and of itself a negative condition. It is simply a symptom that reveals our need for the only remedy—an outpouring of God's reviving presence.

God, in his mercy and grace, may let men sink to this point of despair. He can then be revealed as their only help. Though the pain of alienation from God may appear severe, it is soon swallowed up in the joys of revival.

Drury Lacy on another occasion explained that God uses hardship to produce better Christians. He said, "You know the love a parent has for a child. Now if a child is sick and requires [medicine], the parent will force it down however disagreeable it may be to the taste. God loves his children with a love infinitely more tender than any parent does his child, and he will take care of the health of the soul, whatever sufferings it may cost the body. O, that we might be converted and become as little children to take what is given without resistance."[14]

The church can and must experience revival. We are beyond the days of revival as an option. This outpouring of God's presence is needed today more than ever before. Our churches are barren of the fruit of the Spirit and our baptismal waters are eerily tranquil. Only a heaven-sent, Spirit-led revival will do for these times of satisfaction with the status quo.

"We hear much of the need of revival, and truly the need is great. Real revival can be brought about only by adherence to the Word of God. There may be an ephemeral emotion, a transient zeal, an ebullition of religious fervor and sentiment, but what is acceptable to God, and therefore of real and permanent value, is a return to His will as revealed in the Scriptures of truth. When the psalmist prays, 'Wilt thou not revive [or quicken] us again; that Thy people may rejoice in Thee?' and pleads for mercy and salvation he goes on to say, 'I will hear what God the Lord will speak.' There lies the secret of spiritual reviving."

— W.E. Vine —

CHAPTER TWO

A CHANGE NEEDED

Change is always a difficult subject to discuss. Most of us would prefer everything stay as it is, but this is not possible. The only parts of creation that never change are those that are dead. The church is a living organism and must change or it too will die—or at least it will die as we know it today.

The change that is necessary must come from the inside or the church will be forced to change from the outside. An increasing number of adults in the United States are choosing the concepts and values that appeal to them most. For example, approximately two out of three Americans believe the following:

1) There is no absolute truth.
2) All religions pray to the same god; they just use different names
3) The purpose of life is to enjoy oneself and to reach personal fulfillment.[15]

With beliefs such as these, you can see quickly how a change is needed. The members of our churches are being molded into the world's shape. The Bible is clear on this subject. "Adulterers and adulteresses! Do you not know that friendship with the world is enmity with God?" (James 4:4).

The church can no longer exist in its status quo state, because there is no longer a status quo. We simply cannot wait any longer to institute a change in how we are doing things.

The Church Must Get Right

What exactly is meant by this phrase, "Get right."

It seems that those outside of the church may have a better idea of this than those who warm the pews of the local church each Sunday morning. The youth seemed to be acknowledging the need for revival decades ago in this country.

Though this will date me and leave some scratching their heads, I will reach back a ways and recall a rock group named Credence Clearwater Revival. Not only did they have revival as part of their group's name, some of their song lyrics almost preached the reality of getting right.

Here's the lyrics of one song this band sung. The title of the tune is "Bad Moon Rising."

I see the bad moon arising.
I see trouble on the way.
I see earthquakes and lightnin'.
I see bad times today.

Don't go around tonight,
Well, it's bound to take your life,
There's a bad moon on the rise.

I hear hurricanes ablowing.
I know the end is coming soon.
I fear rivers over flowing.
I hear the voice of rage and ruin.

Don't go around tonight,
Well, it's bound to take your life,
There's a bad moon on the rise.
All right!

Hope you got your things together.
Hope you are quite prepared to die.
Looks like we're in for nasty weather.
One eye is taken for an eye.

Don't go around tonight,
Well, it's bound to take your life,
There's a bad moon on the rise.

Don't go around tonight,
Well, it's bound to take your life,
There's a bad moon on the rise.

These words written by John Fogerty paint a bleak picture of the times. One verse in particular caught my attention:

Hope you got your things together.
Hope you are quite prepared to die.
Looks like we're in for nasty weather.
One eye is taken for an eye.

Right there is a call to get things right. Like the prophet's words to Hezekiah, "In those days Hezekiah was sick and near death. And Isaiah the prophet, the son of Amoz, went to him and said to him, 'Thus says the Lord: 'Set your house in order, for you shall die, and not live.'" (2 Kings 20:1)

It's time for the church to get right. She must get her house in order. Whether she lives or not is immaterial. Doing this is prerequisite to revival coming.

Revival can only start with the church, but the church must ready herself. A restoration of right thinking based on biblical principle is a necessity. The church at Ephesus was fervent with activity, but those people had left their first love (Revelation 2). A renewal of our priorities and a burning love for Christ are needed for revival. We must be aware of what we need to do in getting ready for revival blessings.

Often today we find the church behaving like the world. The revivalists of the last century used the forceful and direct preaching of God's word to arouse the conscience of the church. These preachers of the gospel demanded behavior of the church members that correlated with their talk.

They sought from the church a rejection of worldly values and materialism, regular attendance at religious services, and a model of self-denial that is missing from modern times.[16] The pulpit must again resound with a clear message, "Church get right!"

When revival happens it always happens to individuals. The church cannot experience revival without the lives of individuals being altered significantly.[17] One evidence of real revival is the unquestionable change in behavior.

Throughout scripture, when revival came, reform of lifestyle followed closely. If a person refuses to change they will not be received by the Lord. Cain refused to bring the correct sacrifice and was rejected by God (Genesis 4). Esau would not reject the fleshly desires of his heart. When confronted with the error of his ways, he choose disobedience (Hebrews 12). David, however, repented promptly when Nathan confronted him (2 Samuel 12). He experienced revival.

While the New World of America was being settled, the effects of the Puritan Awakening were significantly noted. In Virginia, laws were enacted which demonstrated the effects of revival upon society.

The Laws, Divine, Moral, and Martial (1610) prescribed severe penalties against cursing, speaking against the Christian religion, and failure to attend church. The laws were expanded in 1619 to include idleness, gambling, drunkenness, and excess in apparel.[18] Not only would the American Civil Liberties Union (a totally anti-Christian organization) not stand for such laws today, but many members of local congregations would revolt.

Another revival which swept through New York state in 1725, produced similar results. Elders and deacons of the local congregations were converted one after another. People were added to the church rolls that had never been in church before. The people were noted as becoming a very different people. Their conversion experience, as a result of revival, left them with a passionate determination to make the attainment of their highest moral ideals the dominating purpose of their lives.[19]

Repentance then is the real change that is needed in the church. Is it necessary to speak of real repentance? Second

Corinthians 7:10 states, "For godly sorrow produces repentance leading to salvation, not to be regretted; but the sorrow of the world produces death." The church has settled for repentance to some degree, which is actually an impossibility. Repentance effects total surrender and the net results is a changed lifestyle.

At a meeting of the Bethel Baptist Association of South Carolina in 1802, a message was preached which confronted the churches with their present state:

> *Brethren, what can we expect, if we live in disobedience, if we backslide in heart and depart from God? Will he not chastise us with the rod of blindness and barrenness? Can we expect anything but a declension? Is it not owing to such conduct that our congregations from year to year complain of coldness and deadness... The truth is, we do not cry to him with sufficient faith: we are too much at our ease: we see cause for lamentation, but we do not lament. It will not be better with us until we alter our conduct and reform our lives.*[20]

These people had come to a full understanding that their present lifestyles had to change both as an antecedent to revival and as an evidence that revival had taken place.

Clear Lines Need to be Drawn

No longer is the line of distinction between the church and the world clearly drawn. The world has pressed in upon the church and slowly a transformation has taken place. It shows only as a dimple here and a crack there, but the church is giving way to the thinking and morals of society.

We are becoming a thermometer instead of being the thermostat of society. Revival is needed if this condition is to be remedied.

A recent Gallup Poll, commissioned by the Southern Baptist Convention, has found that only one in ten Americans considers himself deeply committed as a Christian. Gallup said that based upon his findings most professing Christians in the United States are ignorant of the basic teachings of the faith. They lead lives that are not significantly different from non-believers. Their lack of knowledge makes them most vulnerable to cults and non-Christian philosophies.[21]

It does not take a poll to come to these conclusions. A visit to the local church will provide the same details. What could never be heard even in the back hallways of the church is now openly proclaimed from the pulpit. It may not be disclosed as a distinct point in the pastor's outline, but it is declared loudly by the exclusion of its ridicule!

We must consider what it will take to draw men back from the "gray" areas of everyday life. Unfortunately, or fortunately, according to your perspective, it may take a crisis.

A pattern develops as one studies God's Word and as history is brought into focus. The book of Judges is a classic example of the people of God moving from disobedience to repentance to revival. Each time they cried out to God, it was precipitated by a crisis.

History gives us an example of hard times bringing men back to the reality of revival blessings. During the mid-1800's, an economic depression prevailed over America. Because of this crisis, all denominations recorded gains in membership and a resurgence of commitment to religious ideals. The Methodists alone added over a quarter of a million members, a growth rate of nearly thirty percent.[22]

Most ministries of that day accepted the positive impact of the economic distress. Multitudes of happy and thoughtless persons had to consider their ways, since they had been stripped of all their worldly goods.[23]

Economic disaster appears on the horizon for the world today. The United States alone is amassing multi-trillion dollar debts. When the due date arrives on this massive debt, the church must be ready to receive those who will be driven back to the foot of the cross.

Let us pray that the hearts of men are not too calloused. Let us pray that God will grant one more overwhelming outpouring of His revival blessings.

Whatever it takes, the Christian must again become a light in the midst of a wicked and perverse generation (Philippians 2:15). The lines of distinction have long been marred with the carelessness of loose living. If the church is going to make a difference, the church will have to be different. We need only to remember that the church is not a brick and mortar building—it is us.

Revival is the only answer for today. The church cannot make a difference in her present condition. Our lukewarmness must be infused with the steam of Holy Spirit unction. Let us be a peculiar people again (1 Peter 2:9)

CHAPTER THREE

HEARERS TO DOERS

We live in a day of hearers. The typical person in one of our congregations today might be labeled an "armchair Christian." Many attend church with little intent of applying the information gained from preaching and teaching. Unless the facts are instilled into the fiber of their everyday living, they can make little difference.

The truth needed to live the Christian life is like computer software lying on the desk in front of a computer. Instructions contained on the media are loaded onto the computer's hard drive. The function of that software is to await commands by the user which are then obeyed by the computer's processor. There is no action if the instructions are not given, or if they are not followed.

We need doers, and doers are a product of revival in the church.

Revival Results in Action

Einstein's law of relativity states for every action there is an equal and opposite reaction. With a stretching of application, this principle can be applied to revivals as well.

As revival prompts the believer into action, the believer then becomes an inspiration to others in the congregation. These newly inspired and motivated believers are then compelled to become active. The individual becomes his own "church" as he yearns to share his experience. He begins to perform the duties of the Great Commission on a personal level.[24]

For some unknown reason we are afraid to use the term inactive. We have labeled those on our rolls with a myriad of terms such as, adults away, or non-resident. The reality is, they are, in truth, inactive. Many times a form of spiritual rigor mortis has overtaken them.

During the Second Great Awakening (1790-1865), the church was re-activated. The result was a two-fold increase in Protestant church membership. The pressures of revival intensified upon the un-converted church member as well as the inactive member. This action of revival moved the congregational hearer to commitment.[25]

Revival is a necessity to the daily life of the church. We cannot function without its power and influence. The pew is not the only place in the church that needs revival, however. The pulpits need a fresh touch from heaven also.

A dry, barren pulpit will result in drought overtaking the pew. The preacher is like clouds and wind without rain (Proverbs 25:14). Activity in the minister's life is a prerequisite to activity in the church member's life. This work is not done for the sake of busyness, but is done as a result and response to revival in the heart of the man of God.

Periods of spiritual drought are not uncommon, however. All of us will experience dry seasons in our lives, but we must always look to the refreshing rains of revival. A Georgia Presbyterian confided in 1795, "I seem to labor in vain. God help me. I am dull and languid myself, and I verily believe, the people and I am mutually affected and influenced by each other in that respect."

A Virginia Baptist of this era observed, "Seldom do we see a dull preacher, and a lively church, or vice versa. Therefore, for the most part, to reform the ministry is to revive the church."[26] The church awaits revival...let it start in the pulpit. If you are a pastor reading this revival manual, then let it begin in **YOUR** pulpit!

The action that results from revival may not always be received with open arms. Revival brings drastic change to lives and to church dynamics. Someone said that we have accepted the abnormal as normal for so long that, if we experience the normal, we think it to be super-normal. The super-normal will be the normal in the midst of a people experiencing revival.

History seems to clearly record that each time God moves with supernatural revival power that hell moves against that activity. Could it be that we resist a move of revival because we know deep down that its coming will surely start a war of sorts?

George Whitefield came to America as a revivalist of the eighteenth century. His revival preaching swept across the land and disturbed those who had grown accustomed to no change and little growth.

The churches actually divided into what was known as the Old Sides and the New Sides. This division fell distinctly along the battle lines that were produced as a result of revival.

These Old Side preachers and congregations, because of a lack of vision, lost an excellent opportunity during these days of revival to build their churches. They could have become a part of this revival movement and helped to turn around the moral decay of that time. The people were awakening and in their hour of warmth, these ministers could only fill their pulpits with denunciation of Whitefield, Tennent and others who promoted the awakening.[27] Revival will always result in action, but remember that sometimes those actions may be negative.

Positive Results of Revival

The most noted result of revival is often the committed Christian now involved in a daily walk with Christ. This person will often return to a study of God's Word, prayer, faithful attendance to the house of God, and participation in church activities at every opportunity. More comes from revival than these personal items, however.

The effectiveness of the church in the local community and the world is increased because of revival. This spiritual renewal often results in an increase in giving that allows the church to get to the work of spreading the gospel.

In 1741, George Whitefield presented the work of his orphanages and his desire to build a new tabernacle in London. The products of his revival efforts were the open hearts and the open purses of his listeners. So abundant was the giving that some cried foolishly that the country would become bankrupt.[28] It is not uncommon for a man's billfold to be liberated at an equal rate to his soul's liberation.

The increase in giving by believers allows the church to move out in ever widening circles of influence. The first ripple of influence is a mind for missions. A church in revival immediately begins to contemplate the world outside its own four walls.

The impact of revival focuses upon the next door neighbor, the workmate, the schoolmate, and finally upon all who cross our path. The biblical directives given for winning the world in Acts 1 (Jerusalem, Judea, Samaria, and the world) are still valid today. The only limitation to these directives being carried out is a lack of revival in the land.

We live in a marvelous age of technology. These tools at our disposal allow us to reach distances little thought of in previous generations. The revivals of the last few centuries give us firm evidence, however, that missions are a result of revival in the life of the church.

The Great Awakening of the eighteenth century established many missions.[29] Some of these early mission efforts have lasted through two centuries. Other contemporary missions have been built upon the foundation of these works.

One hundred years before the Civil War, Whitefield was decrying slavery. The common thread of humanity tied both the white and the black together as they wept under the conviction of the Holy Spirit. New insight into racial and social differences were resolved because of revival.

The American Indian benefited from the revival efforts of the Great Awakening. As revival swept over New England, the Indians were caught up in its wake. Jonathan Edwards came into direct contact with the Indians of New York state and they were influenced for Christ.

Whitefield carried news of the Indians back to England and considerable aid came to Indian missions through news of the revival in America.[30]

Perhaps, David Brainerd is most noted for his work among the Indians. Brainerd's ministry was a direct result of revival. His missionary journeys were in the provinces of New Jersey and Pennsylvania.

From March to November of one year he travelled three thousand miles. The successive revivals of this period brought multitudes of Indian bands together under Christ. Such were his efforts that many of the neighboring pastors heralded the Indian converts before their congregations as examples of piety.[31]

Many of the missionary organizations of today have their beginnings as a result of the revivals that spread across the land during the Great Awakening. Some of them are still in existence today. Among the more important of these associations were the Home and Foreign Mission Society (1812), the American Bible Society (1816), and the American Tract Society (1826).

The words of Gamaliel in Acts 5 carry great weight when responding to the results of revival. "And now I say to you, keep away from these men and let them alone; for if this plan or this work is of men, it will come to nothing; but if it is of God, you cannot overthrow it—lest you even be found to fight against God." (Acts 5:38-39)

Revival will give us hearers who do what they have heard. Through a renewed spirit and enlightened heart, they will march for Christ in a darkened world. The results will be unmistakable and the tide of influence will not be stopped.

CHAPTER FOUR

A BIBLICAL BASIS

Revival is no dreamed up fantasy of some preacher or denomination. The basis for revival is firmly fixed in the text of the Bible. From Adam's fall until today, God has been in the "reviving business." We need only study the content of the biblical history to find the truths about revival and its effect upon humanity.

We are in good company when we base our understanding of revival in the context of the Bible. The Puritans held a view of life that came directly from the pages of the Bible. Every facet of their daily living found meaning in the Word of God.

The most significant belief held by the Puritans was the conviction that the Bible held all the answers to life's questions. The Bible, for the Puritan, was the authoritative resource as they responded to the needs of human and social order.[32]

A distinct connection can be drawn between the absence of revival and the proliferation of liberal theology. Revival happens more frequently in congregations that adhere to the infallible Word of God. Our churches will prosper when we return to the instruction of the Scriptures.

Liberalism and its inherent doubt concerning inerrancy is nothing new. More than one hundred years ago a serious challenge to the faith arose in Europe and America. The fallacy of German higher criticism began to sweep the churches.

The attacks that had come from without had been well repulsed, but this attack came from within the ranks. This liberal theology gave natural and rational explanation to the miraculous. The historicity of the Scripture was challenged as myth.

Conservatives of that day grew nervous as they were thrown into a defensive posture. Only an infallible Bible, read by every man for himself, will produce a religious experience conducive of revival.[33] An infallible Bible is still central to revival and evangelism.

Revival and evangelism are closely linked, however, they should not be melded into one concept. They are both operations of, in, and through the church.[34] Paul Rees said, "Revival is an experience in the Church; evangelism is an expression of the Church." The church revived will evangelize.

Throughout the Bible, a pattern develops in which the fervency and commitment of believers grows or wanes. The book of Judges is a classic example of this. The children of Israel would turn away from following God's word during times of prosperity. Time after time as soon as economic distress or calamity overtook them, they would cry out once again to God.

This pattern continued after the completion of the Canon, the generally accepted 66 books of the Bible. Nearly, two thousand years have transpired since Calvary and still these cycles of restoration and revival occur.

Whitney Cross believes that revival occurs in direct correlation to the business cycle. As the business cycle booms, the occurrences of revival decline. When recession or depression occurs, revival flourishes.[35] One does not have to agree fully with such analogy, but the fact remains that men are inclined to forget God in good times.

The Bible yields abundant accounts of revival. Both the Old Testament and the New Testament record periods of renewal and religious vigor among God's chosen people. Some of these accounts will be discussed in the next few sections.

Revival Under Samuel

Revival might be defined as God on the scene. The children of Israel considered the Ark of the Covenant to be the icon of God's presence. It was upon this Ark that the yearly sacrifice of atonement was offered. The Ark rested securely in the Holy of Holies, a part of the Tabernacle enclosure.

While Samuel served as prophet, the sons of Eli contrived a method of defense for Israel. They thought that God would give victory if they brought the Ark into the battle against the Philistines. Little did they know that the Ark of the Covenant had no power of its own. Without the presence of God, it was nothing more than a box of religious relics.

The Ark was carried into battle and lost to the Philistine army. The Philistines suffered much while the Ark was in their presence. The Philistines loaded the Ark on a new cart and sent it back toward Israel. These heathen people responded to God's presence as some churches do. When God's presence is on the scene, a change must take place.

Since there was a requirement to change their lifestyle, they found it easier to send the Ark away. Many churches today would prefer sending God away, than experience the change that comes from revival.

The Ark remained in the home of Abinadab for twenty years. For these years, the people of Israel lamented the loss of the Ark and cried out for God's presence. Their lamentation was not enough to prompt a change in their lives, however. They continued to live contrary to God's law.

Samuel spoke to Israel in 1 Samuel 7:3 saying, "If you return to the Lord with all your hearts, then put away the foreign gods and the Ashtoreths from among you, and prepare your hearts for the Lord, and serve Him only; and He will deliver you from the hand of the Philistines." Samuel knew that revival comes to a prepared people.

A price must be paid to enjoy the freshness of revival rains. This is not an indication that revival can be bought. God cannot be bribed into pouring out revival upon His church, but there must be a travail of heart. God is looking for a repentant people who can receive the blessings of revival. Leonard Ravenhill said there are no sale days at God's revival counter. The cost is always the same—travail.[36]

The people of Israel did pay the price for revival. They put away their strange gods and sought God with all diligence. They repented of their sins and fasted in preparation for the Lord's coming (1 Samuel 7:6). In the remainder of this seventh chapter of 1 Samuel, we find that God did return to this people and their enemies were overcome.

The church will only overcome her enemies when we seek God's face again. Our false gods will have to be put away and our sin confessed, but the reward will be the lifting of our Ebenezer stone (1 Samuel 7:12). Upon this rock of help, we will find revival blessings.

Revival on Mount Carmel

Revival always seeks the most inopportune times to reveal itself. God is always waiting in the wings of time to reveal Himself fresh and anew to his people. It was no different in Elijah's day.

The nation of Israel suffered under the rule of Ahab and his wife Jezebel. The people had turned from worshipping Jehovah God and were now involved deeply in Baal worship.

Elijah came upon this scene with the Word of God as the centerpiece of his message. This word of correction and challenge became the firebrand of revival among a people long dried out from the drought of false religion.

First Kings 18 records the challenge between the prophets of Baal and Elijah on Mount Carmel. The contest was to be decided by the god who answered prayer by fire. With all of their strength, the prophets of Baal appealed to their false gods. Even after cutting themselves and throwing themselves upon the altar, the gods of Baal were silent.

Elijah suggested this contest to prove God's faithfulness and to provoke the people to decision. His words ring clear and true for the church today. From that lofty peak that seems so far removed from us we hear his challenge. "And Elijah came to all the people, and said, 'How long will you falter between two opinions? If the Lord is God, follow Him; but if Baal, follow him.' But the people answered him not a word." (1 Kings 18:21)

Elijah made preparations for the revival fires by restoring the broken down altar. Repairs will always be necessary to the altars of our lives before we can experience revival.

He then made the challenge even more difficult by drowning the altar and the surrounding area in water. He wanted everyone to know that the fire of revival falls from heaven and not by men's design or manipulation.

Elijah's prayer was simple, direct, and to the point. "Hear me, O Lord, hear me, that this people may know that You are the Lord God, and that You have turned their hearts back to You again." (1 Kings 18:37)

The simplicity of revival resounds in this one sentence prayer. Charles Finney said that God is one pent up revival.[37] When all is made ready, God will not hesitate to rain his blessings of rain from heaven's bounty.

First Kings 18:38 tells us that the fire did indeed fall from heaven. God answered Elijah's prayer and consumed the sacrifice, the wood, the stones, the dust, and the water in the trench. Revival fires once ignited consume everything and everyone in their path. Some are consumed to glory and some are consumed to destruction.

A letter written in 1801 tells of a Kentucky revival. The writer stated, "In some it appears like a fire that has been long confined—bursting all its barriers, and spreading with a rapidity that is indescribable...it may be truly said, that the Lord is doing great things for us."[38]

Oh, that the church could again experience the days of Elijah or even the days of the 1801 Kentucky revival. It is time for another Mount Carmel confrontation.

Pentecostal Revival

Leonard Ravenhill spoke boldly of the imperative nature of revival. He said, "Revival is imperative, for the sluice gates of hell have opened on this degenerate generation. We need (and we say that we want) revival. Yet, though slick, shallow saints of this hour would have heaven opened and revival delivered on the slot-machine method, God has not mechanized His glorious power to fit our time-geared religious machinery."[39]

Ravenhill understood the necessity of waiting upon the Lord. Jesus promised that the disciples would receive power for the work that lay ahead of them. That work entailed the complete evangelization of the world. This task was difficult at the least and made possible only with the power of revival at one's disposal.

In Acts 2, we find the Day of Pentecost had come. The disciples had been in prayer and fasting as they awaited the promised power from heaven. Perhaps as important as their prayer life was the sense of fellowship in this place. They were all with one accord in one place (Acts 2:1).

God burst in on this scene with power that violently shook the place. The sights and sounds of this occurrence had never been experienced by these disciples of Jesus and have to this day never been repeated.

A rushing wind swept the room and tongues of fire contacted each one in this upper room (Acts 2:3). These disciples, who for ten days had experienced the absence of their Lord and Master, were now filled with the Holy Spirit (Acts 2:4). The promised power had come and they were equipped to perform the commands left by Jesus at His ascension.

This Pentecostal experience is the essence of revival. A person or a church that comes together in one mind and spirit can seek God's face. They can experience revival and when they do so, the results will always be the same. Souls will be saved and the church will have people added to its number daily (Acts 2:47).

The revival on the Day of Pentecost is not centered on the new tongues. That issue alone is prohibiting revival probably more than any other. The revival of that day was centered on God's presence. When God arrived on the scene in power and glory, revival happened.

The revival which spread through the southern states in the early eighteen hundreds, had the fervor of Pentecost. Crowds gathered nightly to hear the gospel proclaimed. A sense of God's presence was made very clear by the sights and sounds of those revival meetings.[40]

The church can experience revival glory again. We need only study intently God's word and approach the subject of revival from a biblical standpoint. God, who never changes, will again pour out His blessings of revival upon our dry and thirsty souls.

CHAPTER FIVE

THE HISTORICAL RECORD

Abraham Lincoln once said, "Fellow citizens, we cannot escape history." He was right and we shall not attempt to do so. History holds in its darkened recesses a cache of valuable resources for revival today.

Some would challenge the impact that revival played in the formation of this country. However, we need only make a shallow dig beneath the surface of America's past to see revival's effect in the laying of the foundation. Here, we find the influence of revival and the revivalists who ministered in this land. Much of what we do in revival today is owed to their labors.

Someone has said that the men who make history have not time to write it. We can be thankful that the activities of these men of God has been recorded. A broad look into the major outbreaks of revival in recent history will reveal much light for the church today.

In this chapter, the history of revival will be examined as a basis for our present revival activities.

The Great Awakening

The Great Awakening came to America after the Puritan influence had waned. The country was growing rapidly and many who moved westward were not of a religious mindset. This time of revival freshness was actually an overflow of an even larger movement that had spread throughout the British Empire. It had largely begun as a Methodist revival movement.

Colonial society was completely changed by the stirring of this awakening.[41] The effects of this revival among the colonial settlers may be seen in the unified efforts of the Revolutionary War. God's grace had brought freedom to men's souls and these men now sought political freedom.

The Presbyterian and the Baptist denominations were the direct recipients of the blessings of this revival. Their congregations were strengthened by the preaching of revivalists and pastors. These congregations were almost unanimously on the patriot side of the war. The English often sought the Presbyterian and Baptist churches as hotbeds of revolutionary ideas. The meeting-houses were burned and their pastors were charged with treason.[42] All of this external attack unified and strengthened the church for the cause of freedom.

The impact of the Great Awakening can be seen in the framing of our government. The authors of the constitution were directly influenced by revival. Revival among God's people prompted evangelism and heightened the emphasis of holy living.

Our nation was conceived in the midst of these high moral ideals. It was built upon biblical directives propagated by the power of revival preaching.

Whitefield's Influence

The awakening of colonial America was primarily the work of itinerant preachers. These men of God brought a new direction and new style to the preaching of the gospel. Men were called back to a right relationship with God.

When these men appeared on the scene, church membership in colonial America was gained by social status or by mere application to the church. These new style preachers inspired men to a living relationship with God through Jesus Christ. Church membership was made dependent upon this intimate relationship with Christ.

At one point, in the beginning of the awakening, these roving preachers and revivalists stirred the emotions of the people to a fervor. The established churches and their pastors were very alarmed by this movement. They even called on local authorities to stop the work of these preachers.

George Whitefield began his ministry in the midst of this itinerant movement. Some have said that he was the major contributor to the itinerant preaching of the gospel.[43]

Whitefield brought to the revival effort a charisma that easily affected the masses. At twenty-three years of age, he brought strength for the rigors of ministry. His strength and vitality had a broad appeal to the colonial population. His preaching style was filled with singing, arm waving, storytelling, weeping, and praying.

Whitefield brought a personalization of the gospel into his ministry and work. People had been bound in the traditions of the institutional church for a long time. These men proclaimed that church members could now experience a personal relationship with God.

The revivals of the early to middle eighteenth century brought a return of gospel preaching that demanded a real conversion. The church had been filled over the previous century with people who were unconverted. It was correct and proper to be a member of the church. Many were baptized into the local congregation at the request of parents. Any person of social standing would conveniently be added to the rolls of the church.

Thousands came to know Christ as Savior during the Great Awakening. Isaac Backus' conversion is one such testimony of grace. Backus was a young farm boy during 1741 when he heard George Whitefield proclaim the message of Christ.

This young man had attended church, learned a proper catechism in public school, prayed regularly, and was expected to be a member of the church. The church, where his parents attended, did not require conversion as a prerequisite to church membership. Backus wrote of his life, "I lived a careless and secure life for more than seventeen years, though in all this time I did never think that I was converted, but flattered myself with this, that I would turn by and by."

Upon hearing Whitefield and others preaching, he realized his desire to be saved. He did not know how to go about it, however. A letter that Backus wrote after his conversion details the experience and the effect of gospel preaching in a revival setting. Backus penned the following:

Although I was often warned and exhorted (especially by my godly mother), to fly from the wrath to come, yet I never was under any powerful conviction till the year 1741. When it pleased the Lord to cause a very general awakening through the land.... Before these times I never thought myself in a safe state yet eased myself with purposes of turning to God by and by when I should have a more convenient season. In May and June 1741, God by his spirit was pleased in infinite mercy to bring eternal things near to my soul and to show me the dreadful danger of delays.

Nothing now distressed me more than to find that hearing the most powerful preaching and also shrieks and cries of souls under concern did not affect me as I desired, but my heart felt hard notwithstanding. But in truth the Lord was then letting me see something of the plague of my heart and the fountain of corruption that was there...; thus, I worried for some weeks.

On August 29, 1741,...I was mowing the field alone.... It appeared clear to me that I had tried every way that possibly I could and if I perished forever I could do no more—and the justice of God shined so clear before my eyes in condemning such a guilty rebel that I could say no more—but fell at his feet.

I saw that I was in his hands and he had a right to do with me just as he pleased. I lay like a dead, vile creature before him. Just in that critical moment, God, who caused the light to shine out of darkness—shined into my heart with such a discovery of that glorious righteousness which fully satisfied the law that I had broken, and of the infinite fullness that there is in Christ to satisfy the wants of such a helpless creature as I was...that my whole heart was attracted and drawn after God and swallowed up in admiration in view of his divine glories.[44]

We need a restoration of gospel preaching in our land today. With solid gospel preaching, we might see others finding the same God that Isaac Backus found. If George Whitefield were to begin his ministry again today, he would find conditions very similar to those of Isaac Backus' day.

Revival is needed and it must begin in the pulpit. The simple gospel message must resound from the church again. The breezes of renewal will blow and we will experience the freshness of revival rains.

Edward's Influence

Jonathan Edwards stood at the forefront of the First Great Awakening. Edwards' ministry began while spiritual drought plagued America. He was not alone when he described the blessings of revival as "a surprising work of God."

Unrest and spiritual dissention prevailed. Edwards and most Americans believed they were nearer the judgment of God than the mercy of God.

The population of the colonies now was near one million. Thirty to forty thousand converts were added to the church in the first four years of this revival. People were coming daily, prompted by a torrential outpouring of the Holy Spirit.

The grace of God was seen working on the most callous of the colonial pioneers. Rejoicing and singing gave evidence of the joy abounding in their hearts. Edwards responded by saying, "Sinners should take hope in the present remarkable and wonderful dispensation of God's mercy."

This was the time of Edwards' personal revival of heart and ministry. Moved to despair by the complacency of the church, Edwards sought the Lord's face. One of Edwards' most famous sermons, "Sinners in the Hands of an Angry God", came out of this revival experience.

Edwards confronted his congregation with the truth of a holy and righteous God. He always concluded with the hope of heaven's open gates.

> *And now you have an extraordinary opportunity, a day wherein Christ has flung the door of mercy wide open and stands in the door calling and crying with a loud voice to poor sinners; a day wherein many are flocking to him and pressing into the Kingdom of God...; many, that were very likely in the same miserable condition that you are in, are now in a happy state, with their hearts filled with love to him that has loved them and washed them from their sins.*[45]

Edwards went on. to explain the need for revival among his people. In 1742, he said, "Our people do not so much need to have their heads stored as to have their hearts touched." He spoke of the stony condition of the human heart. "By a hard heart is plainly meant an unaffected heart, or a heart not easy to be moved with virtuous affection, like a stone, insensible, stupid, unmoved, and hard to be impressed."[46]

The revival sermon of Edwards' day spoke to the heart of man. Our preaching must do no less. Unless the heart is transformed, no hope of spiritual recovery will be found among God's people. Both the heart of the unconverted and the Christian need the touch of the Great Physician. The prophet Jeremiah cried out for a physician (Jeremiah 8:22). He sought a healing touch for his people and he knew that touch must come from someone and somewhere beyond himself.

We need men today who know their own limitations in ministry. Men who will seek God's face in prayer and believe that God still wants to revive His people. The pulpit must again be filled with a holy unction and a fire that cannot be extinguished. This is part of, and prerequisite to, revival in our land.

The Great Revival of the South

The latter years of the eighteenth century were noted as a time of spiritual apathy. The effects of the First Great Awakening were now distant in the minds of most people. The country was spreading rapidly west and south and many were leaving family and religious ties behind. These changes presented the first evidences of the need for revival. The Great Revival of the South was being conceived in this spiritual lethargy.

The southern evangelical mind functioned differently from that of the old New England mindset. The preachers and revivalists of this era saw every minute detail of life as ordered specifically by God. Even the spiritual drought of the land was recognized as serving the purpose of God.

Because of this firm belief in God's sovereignty and a consensus of Christ's imminent return, the revivalists had every assurance that God would soon revive his people again.

Faith in prayer, a belief in biblical prophecy, and a will to take God at His word were seen as essential contributing factors of this revival. The frontier farmers and housewives began to turn their hearts and minds toward these subjects. The hand of God began to move in wonder working power as the embers of revival were fanned.

Kentucky felt the first surge of heavenly power. Extraordinary crowds poured out of the countryside to hear the gospel. Entire communities were transformed overnight and the hopes of the faithful were filled to overflow.[47] God had begun a revival of proportions not heard of in those parts.

The revival efforts of the past suffered from a common malady of indifference. This malady affects many of our present day revivals. Often, the revival breaks forth with fervor and excitement, but falls as quickly as it rises. The Great Revival of the South had these same characteristics.

James McGready, a Presbyterian pastor, worked in the beginning of this revival. In 1797, he began as pastor of three congregations in Logan County, Kentucky. McGready began an emphasis on the doctrines of repentance, faith, and regeneration. In the first few months of preaching on these subjects eight or nine had claimed conversion. They began working in the local congregations. By winter of that same year, a general falling away occurred. The previous deadness returned and the net result was zero growth.

God always has a remnant waiting in the wings, however. McGready met with this remnant that had been gathered from his three congregations. They covenanted together to pray for revival and an outpouring of the Holy Spirit. The words of their covenant are inspiring and motivating to us who desire revival in our day.

> *We feel encouraged to unite our supplications to a prayer hearing God, for the outpouring of his Spirit, that his people may be quickened and comforted, and that our children, and sinners generally, may be converted. Therefore, we bind ourselves to observe the third Saturday of each month, for one year; as a day of fasting and prayer for the conversion of sinners in Logan*

*County, and throughout the world. We also engage to spend one
half hour every Saturday evening, beginning at the setting of the
sun, and one half hour every Sabbath morning, at the rising of
the sun, in pleading with God to revive his words.*

These few believers, now covenanted together by prayer,
persevered for the next few months. Little happened to
convince them that God had heard their prayer until July
1798. From July through September of that year,
congregation after congregation fell under the convicting
power of God's Spirit. Other congregations waited with
expectancy for the outpouring in their own churches.[48]

Revival possibilities abound today. We are standing on
ground that is very similar to that of the Kentucky revival.
Many mark this as the beginning of the Great Revival of the
South. A new influx of lay involvement began with this effort
and the first stitches of the Bible Belt were sewn.

It is very possible that God might begin the next Great
Revival in your church or mine. We need only covenant with
Him and with each other. The possibilities are limitless.

Finney's Influence

If Whitefield and Edwards stand out as the proponents
of the First Great Awakening, Charles Grandison Finney
would have to serve that position in the Second Great
Awakening.

His ministry followed the efforts begun during the revival
of 1778-1805. His impact upon revival is more than the
preaching of the gospel. He brought new substance and style
to the meaning of mass evangelism.

Finney brought revival to the major cities of America. His revivalism reached Philadelphia, New York, Boston, and even crossed the Atlantic to affect the British Isles. Finney filled the pulpit with the hope of salvation and assurance. He prompted men to believe that they could and should be saved.

The response to his preaching was so dramatic that many of the established churches and their pastors feared the movement. A meeting between Finney and some of these pastors was held in 1827.

The complaints of the clergy centered on what they termed "new measures." These new ideas included all-night prayer meetings, praying for sinners by name, allowing women to pray when men were present, denouncing the "Old School" ministers as "cold, stupid, or dead," and speaking with an irreverent familiarity with God. These groups could come to no terms of compromise, so they parted their ways. Finney was convinced that he had to meet the people's needs on God's terms alone.[49]

Finney spoke directly and straightforward to all who came to hear him. He regularly used the pronoun "you" in addressing those in the congregations. In small communities he would call sinners by name and respond from the pulpit, "Oh, God smite that wicked man, that hardened sinner....Oh, God, send trouble anguish and affliction into his bed chamber this night...God Almighty, shake him over hell!"[50] Many came to the anxious bench (a recent tool of revivalism in Finney's day) to confess their sins and seek repentance.

Finney was not ashamed to use new measures to reach the masses. He likened the preparation for revival to a politician running for office. "What do politicians do?" he retorted. "They get up meetings, circulate handbills, and pamphlets, blaze away in the newspapers...all to gain attention to their cause and elect their candidate." He continued with his flair for drama and emotion, "The object of the ministry is to get all the people to feel that the devil has no right to rule this world, but that they ought all to give themselves to God and vote the Lord Jesus Christ as the governor of the universe."

Finney knew that revival was more difficult when people were not in attendance to hear the preaching of the gospel. He added his own distinct reasoning to this belief. "New measures are necessary from time to time to awaken attention and bring the gospel to bear upon the public mind."

Finney felt that the results justified his methods. He often said that if any other minister could show him greater results with another methodology, he would gladly adopt it.

Some assume that Finney was in a numbers game. Others would come to the conclusion that he played upon the emotional strings of the heart. Finney never denied the necessity of excitement or emotionalism, but never for their own sakes. His number one goal was to turn men's attention to higher ideals.

It was during the ministry of Finney that the church began to realize the specialized call of the evangelist and the revivalist. The "protracted meeting" also became popular while Finney ministered. These revival meetings would extend over a three or four day period with meetings occurring several times each day. Finney crossed all denominational barriers as he conducted mass evangelistic meeting in tents, large churches, and theaters.[51]

Finney was the first to engage the laity in active revival duty. He organized them into pre-revival prayer groups. He encouraged them to distribute revival placards, arrange local newspaper advertisement, and make door to door visits.

He stressed the necessity of follow-up by the ministers and congregations of the local churches. He hired someone to work with him in the leading of music and singing. Special meetings were held for women and Finney's wife led these groups.

Charles Finney laid the foundation for much of what we do in preparation for revival. His sincerity in reaching people for the sake of the gospel has never been surpassed. His zeal and boldness for trying new methods, without compromising the Word of God, should be adopted by all of us. The time is short for those without Christ and we must redeem it at all cost (Colossians 4:5).

"I can give a prescription that will bring a revival to any church or community or any city on earth.

First, let a few Christians (they need not be many) get thoroughly right with God themselves. This is the prime essential. If this is not done, the rest that I am to say will come to nothing.

Second, let them bind themselves together in a prayer group to pray for a revival until God opens the heavens and comes down.

Third, let them put themselves at the disposal of God for Him to use as He sees fit in winning others to Christ. That is all!

This is sure to bring a revival to any church or community. I have given this prescription around the world. It has been taken by many churches and many communities, and in no instance has it ever failed; and it cannot fail!"

— R.A. Torrey —

CHAPTER SIX

PLANNING FOR REVIVAL

Planning for revival is no different from any other type of planning. It takes time to set the parameters of the plan in place and then the diligence to work the plan. Revival planning is foreign to us because somehow we think that revival should just happen.

We expect that revival must be all supernatural in essence or it cannot be revival. C.E. Autrey when speaking of revival preparation says, "One cannot prepare for revival without considering methods."[52]

We are at a serious disadvantage when we enter a revival effort with no more than a "wing and a prayer." This does not discount the importance of prayer. Instead, it takes into full account that God has often used the agency of man in His work here on earth.

Neither does planning presume upon God. We cannot expect that God has to be a part of all that we have prepared or planned.

Perhaps, the best rule of thumb is to seek God's plan for revival. This should be the basis for all that we do in our work of planning revival. Our prayer should be, "God, help us to get in on Your plan and program." Too often we print the program before God has been invited to the party.

Revival requires three ingredients: people, preparation, and presentation. An empty church building will often be a difficult place to experience revival. Revivals are not the product of spontaneous combustion. L.R. Scarbourough noted that half of Billy Sunday's and Dwight L. Moody's success could be attributed to their preparation and organization.[53] Scarborough added, "Remember—there isn't any easy way to have a good revival. If you would have a great revival in your church, you must make great plans for it."[54]

Since revival is for mankind, we must see to it that men, women, boys and girls are present for all of the services. This takes well advanced preparation. C.E. Matthews, the mastermind of the simultaneous revivals of the 1940's and 1950's said, "preparation is seventy percent of the success of the revival crusade."[55] We can no longer expect to place a sign in the church yard one week before the revival meeting and expect the house to be filled. We must begin our planning weeks in advance.

Once we have filled the building with warm living bodies, we can begin the presentation of the gospel. Any time these three ingredients are placed together the possibility for revival exists.

Time to Schedule

Many churches (especially smaller ones) are locked into very short range planning. Often revival is a last minute project or even a "necessary evil" that has to be dealt with each spring and fall.

If your revival is going to be successful you must allow time for preparation, the meeting, and follow-up to occur. This amount of time will vary from church to church. As a minimum, one year in advance should be considered. If possible extend your planning to two years and allow the time frame to grow from there.

The longer the advance time is, the more opportunities will be available for selection of evangelistic teams, dates, etc. It is critical that the church use the best evangelistic teams available. Since these men and women are often scheduled several years in advance you must allow the time necessary to fit their schedule.

We also must consider the multitude of events that our church families are involved in each day. We expect the members of our church to be faithful and to place their church life ahead of other activities. Unfortunately, this is simply not a fact with many of them.

Many of the younger church members have school age children. These children are involved in sports or other extra-curricular activities. A church will never plan around all of these activities, but do not schedule a revival in direct conflict with the major ones.

For example, it would be an uphill struggle in a small community to plan revival while the local basketball playoffs were in town. The week of the county fair would be a difficult time also. Though we expect a responsive faith life from our members, often we must yield our schedules to get the most effective results from revival efforts.

Time to Budget

Advance time frames also give the church time to budget for the revival meetings. A planned revival will cost more than a "surprise" meeting. The cost of the planning will be repaid over and again in changed lives and souls saved, however.

Given enough time, the church members will be able to prepare for the giving of their time and resources to the revival. With sufficient and proper notice, most church members are willing to do anything the church asks of them.

Revival should become a line item in your church budget. This lets the church know that revival is a priority. The smaller church will, of course, budget less than the larger church.

The amount budgeted should not restrict the expectations for an extraordinary revival. If you must, start small, and decide at that moment that you will add to this budget item each year. The time and money spent in preparation will be well invested resources.

Bill Cathey suggests that the revival committee present a budget request form to the budget committee. This form would include such expenses as mileage or plane fare for the evangelistic team, lodging, meals, publicity, and miscellaneous expenses.[56]

Time to Pray

One of the important teams that will be formed during the preparation stage of the revival is the prayer team. Most of the work of this team will be done before the revival. This group with the support and enthusiasm of the pastor will encourage the congregation to pray for revival.

Many of the old stand-byes of revival preparation are still valid today. The cottage prayer meeting cannot be beat for bringing unity and involvement to the people. A word of caution should be considered here. Do not extend the cottage prayer meetings for so long that the people become weary before the first night of the revival.

It is very beneficial to begin the cottage prayer meetings at church. The churches I have led in the T.E.A.M. Concept have set aside the Wednesday night before revival as "In-Church Cottage Prayer Meeting."

The congregation meets briefly in the auditorium for open requests. After instructions are given, we divide into small groups and meet throughout the classrooms of the church.

In these smaller meetings we direct our prayer toward more specific items and support those in our group with love and prayer. These smaller groups prepare our people for the cottage prayer meetings that follow through the next weekend.. The prayers offered are more specific and our time spent is more concise. In this way, we encourage more people to take part in the prayer meetings.

An effective "prayerparation" is the assignment of prayer partners. Using a simple computer program, we sort and assign all of our resident members names. We always match men with men and women with women. Our youth also take part in this time of prayer. It is not uncommon to have a 16 year old become a prayer partner with a 60 year old. It has been my experience that this adds a whole new mindset to the church as these generational gaps are closed through prayer.

Then using a desktop publisher you can produce prayer partner cards. An example of one of these can be seen below. These are distributed throughout the church at least four weeks in advance of the revival. The partners are encouraged to set a common time for prayer. Many of these prayer partners continue their partnerships after the last day of the revival meeting as life-long friendships are built around praying with and for one another.

We Will Pray for Revival!

We have agreed to pray for

<insert evangelist's name here>,

our pastor, each other,

and for

Revival

in our church and in our

community!

<insert member's name here>

&

<insert member's name here>

Prayer Partner Card

Your prayer effort also may incorporate a women's prayer supper or a men's prayer breakfast. Families can be encouraged to participate together in prayer by making these gatherings mother-daughter or father-son events.

Holidays that occur during revival preparation can be used as special prayer days for revival. Often our attention is turned toward prayer while our church and families are gathered.

Prayer will always be a central aspect in revival planning and preparation. With prayer at work we can expect mighty accomplishments in our revival efforts. Leonard Ravenhill said that prayer is as vast as God because He is behind it. Prayer is as mighty as God, because He has committed Himself to answer it.[57]

With all your being, take time to pray.

"If revival does not come within the church fellowship, it will not come anywhere! If revival does not come in us individually, it will not come in our churches. You can only re-vive those who have been vived in the first place. Revival does not mean to be saved all over again. Revival means that the fires of spiritual fervor, having become only hot embers, are again set burning with fervent, flaming heat."

— Herschel H. Hobbs —

CHAPTER SEVEN

THE T.E.A.M. CONCEPT

Most coaches will agree that their overall team is no stronger than their bench. To win the game you must have those in reserve who can fill the place of the first string players. Those who occupy the bench are still part of the team. Though they may see less time on the playing field, they receive the same advantages as the rest of the players.

The spectator is another breed all together. He usually "knows" more than the coach and can "play" the game better than the all-star. This person will always watch others get dirty and wounded in battle, but they never enter the malaise themselves. No matter how loudly they cheer or complain, they will never experience the privilege of actually playing the game.

The church has a larger playing field than all sports combined. The field upon which the church "plays" encompasses the entire globe. The rules by which the "gospel game" is played are simple…win as many for Christ as we can, until He comes again. At the moment of His return, the game is over.

Our problem as a church is that we do not have a team concept. We often function as individuals. Sometimes, we do not function at all. In many cases we have become nothing more than Christian spectators.

Revival efforts are severely hampered by a spectator mentality. We must engage the laity of the church and make them an active member of the team. Churches can no longer allow paid staff (professional players on the gospel team) to do all of the work of ministry. The lay person often is waiting for the opportunity to work for the Lord. The church is not, however, utilizing this volunteer work force.

These workers must be trained for the jobs that we ask them to perform. Training is the missing ingredient today. Our equipping of believers should be a regular part of the church's ministry.

Charles Lake presently serves as Executive Director of Growth Ministries and Consultant for Discipleship for the Salvation Army Southern Territory. He served as the senior pastor of Community Church of Greenwood, Indiana for 29 years. While serving this congregation, he said of their church's training ministry, "We will not ask you to be involved in any ministry for which we are unwilling to train you to do well."[58]

I have created an acrostic using the word *team*. In this way I can easily present the team concept. This is especially true today since the usage of the word *team* has been overused to the point of becoming meaningless.

By using this simple acrostic, the concept of using teams becomes integral to ministry. Ministry is then accomplished each time a team is formed. As a matter of fact, don't create a team that does not have a ministry function.

Here is the acrostic:

T otally
E xcited
A bout
M inistry

When the lay people understand that the work of revival is a ministry, they will become much more active in the work of revival preparation. Remember though, most teams do not just happen. Often, the team members must be drafted. With the right training and practice time, any size church can develop an effective revival team.

Hand Pick Your First T.E.A.M.

The pastor must decide from the outset of the planning that he will be actively involved. For lack of a better terminology, he must be willing to be the revival coach. This is especially true as you begin the team concept in your church. The membership needs strong leadership during this training stage.

Be bold enough to hand pick your first team. This group will constitute your revival steering team. Begin now to convert your thinking from committee terminology to team terminology. People can be spectators on committees, but they must take an active part on a team.

The disciples in the early church found that they needed the help of the laity. Disputes had arisen over who would care for certain individuals in the church. It appears that even at this early date in the church's existence, some thought that it was the responsibility of the apostles to do everything. The spectators were calling plays from the sidelines!

When this need arose, the apostles gave instructions. "Therefore, brethren, seek out from among you seven men of good reputation, full of the Holy Spirit and wisdom, whom we may appoint over this business..." (Acts 6:3).

This was clearly a call to assemble a team of deacons to take care of this specific detail of ministry. The principle of creating a team for any ministry need can be easily developed from this action as recorded in the book of Acts.

You will need men and women who will be courageous in their team duties. They will need to be faithful in attendance and willing to sacrifice their time and efforts. This is not the time to give someone a job to see what they can do. These key team members will be your first string. Only the best will do.

A chart detailing this revival steering team is included on the next page. A broader discussion of the work of each team member can be found following the organizational chart.

"If this world is going to be reached, I am convinced that it must be done by men and women of average talent. After all, there are comparatively few people in this world who have great talents."
— D.L. Moody —

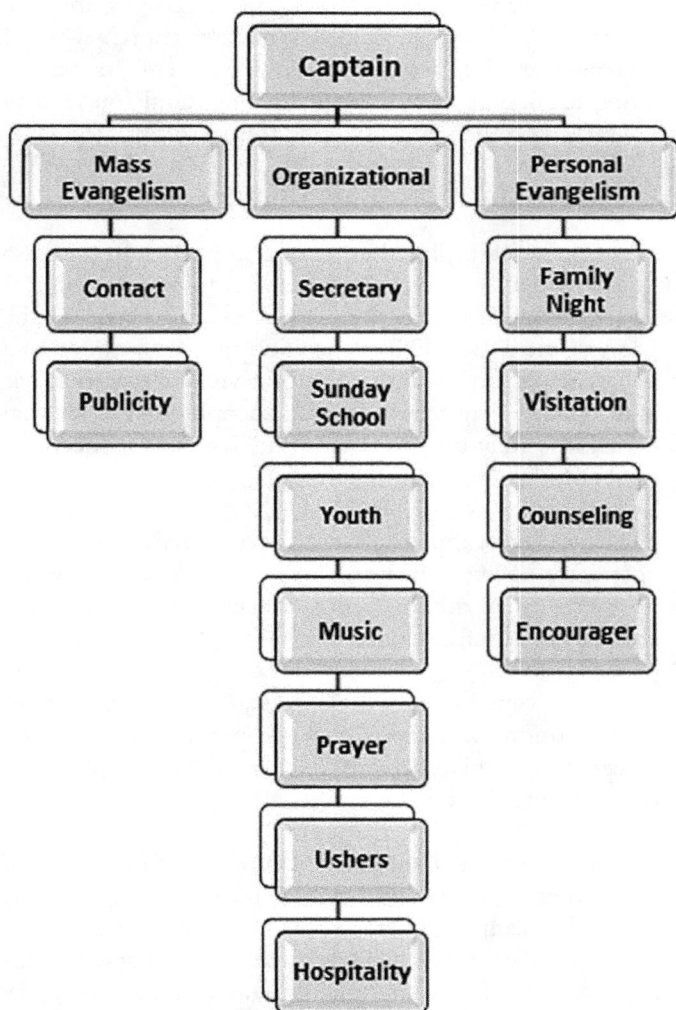

Revival Steering T.E.A.M.

You may adapt the organizational chart to fit the needs of your church. Smaller churches can begin with fewer members on the revival steering team. Duties may be combined and shared if needed. The first church where I began using revival teams had only six members on the steering team. This team eventually grew until fourteen or more served on the revival steering team.

Understanding T.E.A.M. Components

As mentioned earlier, the pastor is important to the team concept. When a church first decides to implement this revival preparation plan, the pastor should serve as the captain of the T.E.A.M. This position may be assigned to a capable lay person, after the idea of revival preparation has caught on in the church, but initially people need to see that the pastor is fully on board with the T.E.A.M. concept of revival preparation.

The pastor or captain will serve as an effective role model as instructor and coordinator. Unless the team members are instructed in their duties, confusion will arise, and much of the work will be left undone.

Since the captain serves as coordinator of all the activities and preparation for the revival, the team members will need to report to this person regularly. This step adds accountability to all involved.

Team leaders will be instructed in the all of the details of revival preparation. It will be their responsibility to guide each of the team members serving in their area toward a successful revival meeting experience. Just as a sports team must have all plays and individual assignments in place before the game begins, each revival team member must know all the processes involved in the revival preparation.

All the team leaders must understand the answers to three questions:

WHAT?

HOW?

WHEN?

Most church members have been told what to do time and time again. They are bombarded from every angle with instructions about their lives, families, finances, etc. Many of these Christians have a desire to work for the Lord. They often find a list of to-do items, but they have no inkling about the final two questions, how and when.

The captain or pastor should make available to the team members the formula for successful revival planning. This formula must be kept as simple as possible. The simplicity of the plan is not indicative of the spiritual depth or mental ability of the team. Keeping it simple makes the work more appealing and more can be done in a shorter time.

Always break large jobs into smaller components. For example, the contact team will be made up of the leader (hand-picked by the pastor) and the players (picked by the leader.) If 150 families need to be contacted by telephone, then ten members are needed on this team.

Instead of two people having the responsibility of calling 75 families, each person will only need to call fifteen. The job gets done and more of the membership is involved in the revival. This gives ownership of the revival to the church. People will always take better care of that which they own. Revival is no different.

Each of the team leaders will report to the captain. This reporting will solve the final question of *when*. Most people are accustomed to reporting their progress to someone on their jobs. The church is one place where most people find little accountability.

At least two team meetings will be held before the first day of the revival meeting. Each team leader will give a report to the other team leaders. In this setting, the leaders are responsible not only to the pastor or captain, but also to a group of their peers. If a person comes unprepared to the first meeting, it never fails that by the next week's meeting they will have brought all of the preparation work up to date.

When each participant understands the importance of revival preparation, respective jobs will be done with diligence and zeal. The intention of all of this planning is not to exalt the individual, but to bring glory and honor to the Lord. "Therefore, whether you eat or drink, or whatever you do, do all to the glory of God." (1 Corinthians 10:31)

Each captain should understand that it is not their personal responsibility to get the work done. They should encourage as much participation from the congregation as possible. Always expand the network of "owners" in the revival. Those who work in preparation for the revival will usually be ready to attend the revival.

Three broad divisions make up the team. These can be adjusted, combined, or renamed as the individual church desires. The divisions shown on the previous chart show the areas of ministry involved in revival preparation.

CHAPTER EIGHT

MASS EVANGELISM TEAMS

Mass evangelism deals with reaching as many people as possible with the resources available. Some may consider that mass evangelism is not an option to the small or rural church. If your "masses" only consist of ten people, then reach them all for Jesus. When you do so, you will have been engaged in mass evangelism. If your "masses" consist of metropolitan cities, then by all means reach all of them you can. When you do so, you too, will have been engaged in mass evangelism.

Contact T.E.A.M.

The first person that needs to be chosen to serve as part of the mass evangelism team is the contact leader. Without a relevant list of contacts, the mass evangelism team will be crippled in fulfilling its duties. This person will gather all of the information available on the prospects available in their community and church. These prospects will be divided into three groups:

1) The lost
2) The unchurched
3) The unfaithful

The Sunday School roll is a good place to begin. The information gleaned from these rolls will begin your prospect list. These names will need to be shared with the visitation captain.

A list of prospects can be gathered from those who already attend your church. Several weeks prior to the revival meeting you may distribute throughout the church cards which might be titled: **I Know A Prospect!** A sample of one such card is shown below.

I Know A Prospect!

Name: _____

Address: _____

_____

_____

Phone: _____

Age: ____ **Church member: Yes or No**

If yes, where: _____

Other Information: _____

_____

Prospect Card

The local telephone book can be used as a resource for this team. The pages of the telephone book can be photocopied and distributed to the team members.

Always remember to keep the task small. Divide this work to create as much involvement as possible. I found that senior citizens and shut-ins enjoy working on this team. Often, they have been isolated from the church and the work of the Lord. A calling list of ten to fifteen names, given as an assignment to these people, makes them feel included again.

Publicity T.E.A.M.

We live in a news-oriented society today. Most individuals desire information on many levels. The publicity methods used by the church must be varied to reach as many people as possible. The news of a revival must get to the churches as well as the unchurched person.

Often, we expend large amounts of energy in scheduling a revival and procuring the evangelistic teams. Then, we give little attention to publicizing the meeting. When only a few people attend the meetings, we offer a multitude of excuses. We even conclude that revivals just do not work in this day. The real reason for failure was that no one knew about the revival meeting.

The publicity team will be the news gathering and dissemination arm of the revival. They will get the news of the revival out to the public. Their work will involve promotion of the revival both inside and outside the church.

This team will usually consist of three to five members. Each will have a specific responsibility in revival promotion. These team members should be chosen and have already begun their work no later than six weeks prior to the revival.

Posters should be designed to incorporate the theme of the revival. Since each night of the revival will have a special emphasis, this should be well publicized in the church. The team will find many aspiring artists in most congregations. These people will be able to use their talents in the production of these posters. From time to time we have allowed the children of our church to produce all of the posters. These are then displayed in strategic spots throughout the buildings. These posters should be in place no later than five weeks before the revival begins.

The publicity team will work closely with the youth team. Together, they will canvas the community to distribute revival flyers on the weekend preceding the revival. Our youth often get permission to pass out these flyers to customers at the local businesses. The larger parking lots are filled with autos and several hundred flyers can be placed on the windshields of these vehicles in a very short time. Always get full permission to do this!

Television and radio media are more than helpful in revival promotion. Most radio stations offer free community news spots. Some television stations now offers the same service. With the advent of cable television, inexpensive and widespread advertising has become available. Many cable systems have a community bulletin board station. These services are often free of charge to non-profit organizations.

Newspapers have free space on the religious pages. Paid advertisements are good, if the cost is not prohibitive. This team will learn to find the best promotional ideas for the dollar. As important as promotion is, we must be good stewards.

Check with local banks and other business that have electronic marquees. These companies often will advertise your meeting on their marquees for no charge. Remember that you may not be the only one asking for this privilege, so ask early.

The publicity team also will be responsible for contacting all churches in the area. Letters should be sent to these churches no later than two weeks prior to the revival. Include with the letter a supply of revival flyers. Many churches will promote your revival effort by posting these flyers at their church, listing your revival dates in their bulletins or newsletters, or by attending as a group on one or more nights. The publicity team can be beneficial to the spread of revival from one congregation to another in this way.

Always remember to let the associational office know about the revival meeting. This office will include your information in newsletters and on their website. This will place your information in every church connected with the association.

When I first wrote this book on revival preparation, the Internet was in its infancy. No one had ever heard of Facebook, Twitter, or any of the other popular social media sites that now flourish in the digital world. Texting was what printers did by hand as they laid out the copy of newspapers, magazines, etc.

The smallest church has every capability to easily use these tools to advertise their revival meetings and to do so with absolutely no cost. Facebook pages can be built and people can be encouraged to attend your events right from these sites.

Tweets can be scheduled at regular times throughout the day and automatically posted with tools such as Hootsuite. The great thing about these tools is that they are constantly evolving and are becoming easier to use with each new version.

These electronic tools cause some people to immediately throw up their hands in resistance because of their lack of knowledge. Here's the good news! Every church has somebody in it that knows how to use these social media sites to get the word out about your revival. This is a great opportunity to get young people involved in revival preparation.

You might wish to add another team under the mass evangelism group that will handle nothing but the social media engagement of your revival publicity.

God has given the church of the twenty-first century the tools to reach the world with the gospel. These tools will allow you to be cutting edge while never forgetting that some of the old-school stuff still serves well to get the news out about your next revival meeting.

CHAPTER NINE

PERSONAL EVANGELISM TEAMS

Revival must include personal evangelism. By using the following methods, personal evangelism will already be in place and working when revival comes. This is very easy to expand and modify according to local needs.

Family Night T.E.A.M.

The first team that will be formed under personal evangelism is a family night team. This team will consist of a team leader and those selected by the leader as team mates. With the proper methods, this team can reach a greater number of people for the revival than any other team.

The work of this team is focused on one particular night of the revival meetings. Wednesday night is an excellent night for Family Night activities. Wednesdays are normally a hard day to get people to attend revival. The efforts of this team will eliminate this mid-week slump in attendance.

The team captain should have a team selected at least six weeks before the start of the revival. A list of all families in the church can usually be gathered from the church office or the church clerk. This list should be divided into small groupings so that no person has to contact more than 15 families. Remember to keep all of the work divided into as small of portions as possible.. This gives more people ownership in the revival and makes the work easier for the team members to accomplish.

Every family in the church will receive a personal invitation from this team. This invitation will be sent by postcard and it should arrive in the home about two days prior to the start of revival. A sample postcard is shown below:

Family Night Celebration

You are invited to attend our Revival during <dates here>.
Evangelist <name here> will be with us at
7 p.m. each evening.
We have set aside a special night to honor the families of
our church and community on <date> at 7 p.m.
We will have a great time of fellowship afterwards, in
which, we hope to meet every one of you.
Mark this date on your calendar now and plan to attend your
night here at <church name here>.

If you need more information
call our church office at
<numbers here>.

Your Friend in Christ,
<Team Member's Signature>

Family Night Invitation

The timing of all mailings is very important. Many of the teams will be contacting families in the church and community through the mail. If mailings are done according to schedule, then the news of revival will reach these people day after day in their mail boxes. The repetition of the news of revival will stress the importance of their attendance.

The fellowship that follows the services on family night can be varied from meeting to meeting. Coffee and cake or pie and ice cream are often used by churches. The menu is kept simple so more people will participate in bringing all that is needed.

Remember, the idea is to get people into the building to hear the gospel. A dessert fellowship is wonderful, but it cannot hold a light to the joyous occasion of entire families coming to know Christ as their Savior.

A special recognition can be made during the family night service for the family who brings the most family members on that night. A simple gift such as a photo album or a gift card to a restaurant can be given to honor their efforts of gathering their loved ones into the house of the Lord.

This night has been a wonderful experience over the years that I have used the T.E.A.M. concept of revival preparation. Entire families have joined the fellowship because of these gatherings. This results in immediate growth to the church and in some cases families are rejoined around the altar.

Visitation T.EA.M.

Visitation is never easy. It does not become easier just because it is revival time. If we are going to reach the lost and unchurched, we must visit them where they live and work.

Revival is a perfect time to encourage the church to participate in a visitation program. In some cases, this may be the only time during the year that you can count on people to visit with any level of intensity.

In this day and time both parents work in many families. This presents a problem. It is difficult to expect a working mother or father to drop everything at home and attend a night of visitation. Many of those we visit are in the same category. They do not welcome the intrusion, no matter how righteous the reason might be.

The visitation team can promote visitation on two levels. Regular, organized visitation times can be set for those who can attend during the evenings. Others who cannot attend at these times can be encouraged to participate in market-place evangelism. People can reach others as they go about their everyday business.

Two main nights of revival visitation should be arranged by this team. The team should be established six weeks before the revival begins to ensure time for gathering prospects, etc. This team will be made up of volunteers from the congregation. Each volunteer will be able to sign up for visitation using a card similar to the one shown on the next page.

Don't forget the three questions that must be asked if revival preparation is going to work.

WHAT?

HOW?

WHEN?

Most folks would agree that visitation should be done. Some will even take a step to learn how to go about visiting people for evangelistic reasons. It is the last question of *when* that must be asked. This is where accountability enters the equation.

By signing a commitment card for visitation, accountability deepens from an agreement between two people to a responsibility unto God. The card will remind folks when they should visit and their signature will help to hold them accountable.

The Lord Can Count On Me!

I will take part in visiting for
Revival!

Please circle the dates you will participate

<1st Date Here>   <2nd Date Here>

Visitation Commitment Card

These cards can be distributed during Sunday School and during the worship services. A team meeting can be held for all who have volunteered to serve. This meeting will set the strategy for reaching people for Christ.

The first visitation night should be used to visit non-attending church members. The second night can be used to visit the lost and unchurched in the community.

If possible, the visitation team could help the pastor and the evangelist in visitation during the week of revival. The bulk of the visitation should always be done prior to the beginning of the revival meeting, however. This will ensure that the church will be filled with those who have heard the news of revival coming to their community.

Counseling T.E.A..M.

One of the blessings of revival preparation is the training of men and women for the work of counseling. The counselor team should have as its leader a person who is a diligent soul-winner. This person must be knowledgeable in the counseling ministry, so they can help with the training of others.

Again, this team should be assembled at least six weeks before the revival begins. The team should meet as soon as possible after formation to discuss plans and pray for revival. A meeting of this team will be held one week before the start of revival for final instructions.

The prayer team and the counseling team will work closely together for six weeks before the revival. This team will be defeated at the outset, if they do not rely heavily upon prayer.

No one should be asked to serve on this team if they are not thoroughly prepared. Fortunately, there are many materials available to help in the training of your counselors. One of the best is *The Billy Graham Christian Worker's Handbook*. It can be ordered directed from the Billy Graham Evangelistic Association by using this link: http://www.billygrahambookstore.org/product.asp?sku=21 61_83087.

Billy Graham said in the foreword of the handbook, "As you use this book, you will be encountering people at crucial turning points in their lives—people who, through various circumstances and the prompting of the Holy Spirit, are open as perhaps never before to the Gospel. This *Christian Worker's Handbook* comes to you with my heartfelt prayer for God's blessing as you use it for His glory."

The counselor will face many decisions during the invitation. Often, much more than soul-winning will need to be discussed with the counselee. *The Billy Graham Christian Worker's Handbook* covers many of the common questions that arise during the invitation. Some of these include: salvation, assurance, abortion, abuse, alcoholism, bad habits, bitterness, divorce, doubt, false doctrines, heaven, hell, obedience, patience, prayer, stewardship, temptation, and evil thoughts. The manual offers counseling strategies and scriptural answers. It is a must for the serious counselor.

Another guide used regularly is the *Personal Commitment Guide* which can be downloaded for free from the North American Mission Board's website. Printed copies can also be ordered very inexpensively.

You can use the following link to access information about this product: https://www.namb.net/commitment-guide/ .

This guide takes a step-by-step approach to several of the most common questions that arise at the invitation. Salvation, assurance, baptism, church membership, and rededication are covered. The guide is designed as a tool for the counselor and a commitment card for the counselee. A supply of these should be in the hands of the counselors and available in each counseling area.

PERSONAL COMMITMENT GUIDE

An effective counseling team is essential to seeing more decisions for Christ, as well as, more definite decision making by the counselees. Your counseling team should be instructed to do the following at each invitation:

1) Create movement at each invitation. Some of the counseling team should come forward to the altar for prayer, others should take places near the front of the church for quick access to those making decisions.

2) Some of the team must be ready to take the pastor's place in extending the call for decision. Often, the pastor will need to speak with an individual for a moment. During this lull in the call, many will decide not to come forward. A trained counselor should step forward immediately and continue to extend the call.

3) Counselors should take all counselees to the designated counseling areas. This provides privacy, as well as, an unhurried atmosphere for the counseling session. Counselors should never attempt to force a decision. If the decision comes after the service has closed, the person can be instructed to return to the next service where he can make that decision public.

4) Counselors should not counsel a person of the opposite sex alone. Make sure that two of the counselors join forces. One can conduct the session while the other person prays quietly for the Holy Spirit to work.

The counseling team will have an effective ministry that will extend beyond the dates of the revival. Properly trained, they will be ready to serve at every invitation given during the year. Also, this team will grow as church members become interested in helping others make a decision for Christ.

Each counselor should always be in a mentoring mode. Trained counselors may take an untrained person with them into a counseling session. Nothing can compare with on-the-job training. The confidence of these "counselor-helpers" builds as they experience first-hand the decisions of those who have visited the counseling rooms.

As a person receives this hands-on training their confidence is strengthened and soon a new member is added to the counseling team. As this group works with the Holy Spirit, men will be drawn to Christ and the church will grow both numerically and spiritually.

Encourager T.E.A.M.

The encourager team is synonymous with follow-up. One area that often fails to be addressed is the time of follow-up needed to secure decisions that have been made during the revival. Sometimes we only follow-up on decisions for salvation. This is unfortunate, because the Christian who makes a renewed commitment will need support also.

This team will be the "Barnabas" arm of the revival meeting. Barnabas was noted in the first century church for his gift of edification and encouragement. The encourager team will serve longer than any other team. Their work will begin six weeks before the revival and continue for several weeks after the meetings are over.

An encourager team will be assigned the duties of staying in contact with all who make decisions during the time of the revival meeting. This follow-up will last for a minimum of six weeks after the last day of the revival meeting. During this time, the new convert or the Christian who has made a decision can be nurtured and strengthened.

Encourager Assignment

For the next 6 weeks, I will contact

_____

**at least once a week, so I can be
an encouragement to
them and their family.
My desire is to help them grow as
they become a part of our family here
at
<church name here>
as they follow through on their revival
decision.
Date Assigned: ___/___/____**

Encourager Assignment Card

In smaller churches, the counseling team may also serve as the members of this team. In this way, the relationships established during the counseling times may continue for the next few weeks.

An encourager assignment card will be given to each team member. The card will be a commitment by the encourager to the team that he will follow-up quickly by contacting the person named on the card. An assignment date and completion date will be filled in and the card returned to the encourager team leader. The encourager assignment card may be similar to the one shown on the previous page.

The encourager team will make new converts aware of all church service times and dates. This will assimilate them quickly into the fellowship of the church.

The Sunday School will be the first place you will want to introduce these newest members. It is in the Sunday School that the strongest biblical foundations can be laid. These classes provide a place where the needs of these families can be met. Connecting the individual and the family to age-graded departments assures this will happen. In these departments solid connections will be made that help secure a relationship to the church family.

The Christian who has made a decision during revival will need prayer and support to follow through on that decision. You as a member of the encourager team may be the strongest link to their completion of that commitment. This work of encouraging will cost the price of time and concern for others. The church must realize that real growth is impossible without a solid follow-up program. The encourager team is the answer to this dilemma.

CHAPTER TEN

ORGANIZATIONAL TEAMS

The organizational section of revival planning is the largest of the three sections. The focus of these teams is still centered on bringing people to Christ.

The teams that make up this section of the revival steering organization chart find their beginnings in the everyday activities of the church. These groups will merely redirect their attention while involved in revival planning. Their work will concentrate on involving as much of the congregation as possible in revival activities.

Revival Secretary

The revival secretary will work with all the teams to produce the letters, flyers, calendars, banners, etc. This person could be a paid church secretary, but may be another lay member. In smaller churches, the pastor may need to fill this capacity.

A computer is a beneficial tool for the work of the revival secretary. There are few who do not have ready access to a computer. Even if the church does own a computer, there will usually be someone in the congregation that will provide the use of a personal computer. Here again is another opportunity to incorporate the help of some of the younger members of the church. The hardware, software, and the young people who know how to effectively use them are wonderful assets that we have been given in this day to do the work required in preparation for a revival meeting.

All the sample cards and charts included in this book were created on a personal computer. With the advent of desktop publishing, most of the printing work for the revival can be done in the church office. This greater reduces the costs that used to be prohibitive to small congregations.

Software is available to produce the calendars for each team. These calendars will hold all the planning strategies for the team. Having the dates for implementation and completion clearly explained will make the plans clear. This also will help to prevent procrastination. These calendars will hold the answers to the three questions previously discussed: **what, how, and when**.

Word processors can be used to print form letters that can then be merged with membership addresses. Local churches can be sent letters of invitation by merging letters and addresses. As these letters, postcards, and other mail outs are developed, time can be saved in future revivals by editing recorded forms.

Banners and flyers can be produced on the computer to promote the revival. Special events held during the revival can be promoted using a variety of software.

This person may be trained to maintain a website that will detail all of the revival activities. This can be easily done in a drag and drop fashion with services such as Wordpress.

Social media updates can be the responsibility of the secretary also. Since this person will have such a massive amount of work, it will be good if they find some willing assistants—preferably some that are computer savvy!

The revival secretary is indispensable in preparing for the revival. This person will need to work closely with the revival captain. The secretary must be aware of all the work of each team. With the right training and tools, the secretary will be able to help all the teams do their very best work.

Sunday School T.E.A.M.

Revival can produce a significant growth benefit for the Sunday School. The Sunday School, however, is actually the breeding ground for revival enthusiasm. When the Sunday School team pours its energy into revival planning, some of the best effects of the revival can be experienced in the local church.

During the Second Great Awakening, the church began to realize the potential of the Sunday School. The teaching of the Sunday School had one purpose—the conversion of the soul.[59] In the Second Great Awakening, revivals sprang directly out of the Sunday School organization. The Sunday School was considered the focal point of the ingathering for revival.[60]

The Sunday School team will be under the leading of the Sunday School director. This person will begin work six weeks before the revival to put their team to work. The great thing about this team is that it is already in place and is active each Sunday of the year. You will not have to search very far for those who will be the members of this team. The team simply consists of all the Sunday School teachers.

The main focus of the Sunday School team is high attendance day. To accommodate the observance of this special day requires a change in the revival start date.

Nearly everything that is done in the local church points toward Sunday—except for revival meetings. Why do we begin revival meetings **on** Sunday and move **away** from it?

Nearly all revival meetings have traditionally begun on Sunday and moved away from the normally highest attending day on the church calendar. Participation in the revival meetings then tend to wane toward the last day of the scheduled meetings.

The T.E.A.M. concept of revival preparation requires a change in the beginning day of the revival. The meeting can begin on any weekday that your church decides, but Wednesday is the best. This is a regular meeting night in most churches and a good time to gather families together. *See the previous section on hosting a family night during the revival.*

This may appear awkward to you at first, but with the right preparation you will not need a Sunday morning crowd to begin the meeting. You will have a Sunday morning crowd and more every night of the week.

There are several reasons why the revival meeting should end on Sunday. First, since the meetings will be moving toward a high attendance day the church will have several nights during the revival meetings to encourage people to be in attendance on this particular Sunday.

Always set an attainable goal for the church. It is better to set several goals during the year instead of just one. Set a goal that can be reached easily. The goal needs to be challenging, but always attainable. I have used the "10% rule" for many years. Take your average Sunday School attendance for the past year or your last recorded high attendance and add 10% to it. That would be your goal on high attendance day. I have seen Sunday Schools triple in attendance over a short time using this system.

Second, the people attending the revival during the week will have an outlet for their renewed spiritual zeal. They will be able to invite someone immediately to the church for this special day.

Third, the high attendance day in Sunday School will be a first step of faithfulness for new converts. If there are plenty of visitors and guests in the Sunday School classes on this Sunday, it will be easier for them to feel comfortable.

Fourth, the Sunday School will grow consistently from revival meeting to revival meeting. The church will experience real tangible growth.

One group of teachers will have a special duty during revival preparation. The fourth, fifth, and sixth grade teachers will plan and host the pre-teen rally on one night of the revival.

It is important on this night, as well as youth night, to promote these activities as pre-revival gatherings. If the team presents the pre-teen rally as children's night at the revival, then you will find the adults staying away. The purpose of these special nights is to present the gospel on a level that the children can understand. These children will join their families in the regular services for all age groups.

The pre-teen night will usually begin one hour before the regular start of services. Prepare foods that are easily consumed and not messy. Pizza or nachos are two of the best. The ideal is to have all food served and finished within thirty minutes.

This will leave the concluding part of the hour for the gospel presentation. Be original in this presentation. Movies, clowns, or drama works well. Children need more than the evangelist or pastor preaching for half an hour.

Pre-Teen Rally

This ticket is good

for

Pizza & Fun

at

<Your church, date, time>

You and a friend may enter with this ticket!

Value: $10.00

Pre-teen Rally Ticket

The key to getting the children to attend this meeting is the invitation and tickets they will receive. Children love to receive mail. When it comes from their church it becomes more special to them.

Invitations need to be mailed so they will reach the children two days before the pre-teen rally night. Each child should receive with their invitation a supply of tickets. Note that each child should receive a **supply** of tickets. I would suggest at least 10 for each child.

You probably cannot go onto a school campus to distribute these tickets, but each child can! These tickets can be given by the preteens to all of their friends during the next two days. Make this an important part of the invitation process. With each ticket admitting the preteen and one friend, the potential is explosive.

Also, do not fail to include a value to the ticket. Even though the event is free, the fact that the ticket shows a value will insure that they are not just thrown away. This one little secret will make a huge difference in how many of these tickets are distributed.

The church will be blessed with an abundance of children present for the rally and an opportunity to win many for Christ. An example of the pre-teen rally ticket is shown on the previous page. These can be produced eight to the page and cut for distribution to the children.

Youth T.E.A.M.

The youth team leader will be either the youth director or a youth Sunday School teacher. This team will be formed six weeks prior to the revival meeting also.

One of the functions of the youth team is the distribution of revival literature. On the Saturday before the revival begins, the church youth will visit the homes in your community. Each home should receive a revival flyer. The youth also can hand out (with permission) flyers in parking lots in the community. Many businesses will allow the youth to place flyers on the autos found in their parking lots.

A youth night (remember, this is to be presented as a pre-revival emphasis) will be held during the revival. Friday nights are usually the best for youth night. The emphasis will be two-part for the youth. A pre-revival "pizza blast" or "nacho nonsense" will be held one hour before the revival meeting.

The youth team must concentrate on fresh ideas and concepts for their work. The youth will not attend unless there is evidence of their best interest in place. Our youth are being bombarded on every side by the world. We must show them there are alternatives. This must be done always without compromise and according to the standards of God's word.

The types of activities connected with youth night are too numerous to list, but a few may include: games, Christian illusionist, chalk art, or videos. Talk with your youth. They will be your best sounding board for ideas.

An afterglow will follow the revival meeting. The afterglow is a special time of testimony and fellowship that follows the regular revival meeting. While the youth are assembled in this setting, the gospel can be presented on their level. It is always a good time to follow up on decisions made during the pre-revival activities or during the services. Always have plenty of adult counselors on hand to help with the decisions on this night.

Music T.E.A.M.

C.E. Matthews said that salvation and song are dual in nature. Music has been the inspiration of many past revivals. Dwight L. Moody credited Ira D. Sankey with bringing more people back to God through his music than he did through preaching. Gospel singing stands second only to the preaching of the gospel.[61]

The music team will be headed by the worship leader in your church. He will be joined by the instrumentalists and others in the church that are musically inclined.

The music of the revival should be special in nature. This is no time for the same old tired selections. The older solid hymns certainly should be used, but this is a great time to insert some newer variety of music into the services.

The portion of the service set aside for music should be designed to inspire and prepare the people for the preaching of the gospel. Use of outside help is sometimes needed to achieve this.

Often, the evangelistic team will be able to assist in the presentation of music for the revival. The evangelistic team along with local talent should know that a performance is not being called for in the revival. At all cost the Lord Jesus Christ should be exalted. Give sufficient time for singing, but leave plenty of time for the preaching and invitation.

If a revival choir is to be used it should be solicited in advance of the revival. A full choir will help lead the congregation in singing and will give the appearance of a full church. When space is a problem, the choir will often need to remain in the choir area during the services. A "full house" is one problem most pastors seldom see any more during a revival meeting, but having the church filled is certainly desirous of all. The music team can play a vital part in making sure that many attend the revival.

When more people are asked to participate in the music portion of the meeting, then more people will take ownership of the revival. Use all age groups when considering those who will sing from the platform. This will be an additional guarantee that the families of those singing will be in attendance on that particular night.

Prayer T.E.A.M.

The work of the prayer team has been partially discussed in chapter six. You may turn there for ideas about promoting prayer and to find examples of prayer cards, etc.

One additional duty of the prayer team is to arrange for special prayer and testimony times. These special times of prayer and testimony should begin at least two weeks before the revival begins.

Ask the pastor to allow laymen to have the opportunity of leading in prayer at all services which occur during these two weeks. Those who pray will concentrate their prayer on the upcoming revival. This will promote prayer by the entire church. It will also remind the prayer partners to keep up their efforts.

The testimonies given in this two week period should be given by individuals who have been directly affected by revival. Limit these testimonies to three minutes. A personal testimony should be given at each service held during this two weeks period. Planning will prevent anyone from trying to just ad-lib their testimony. Once again, all should be done for God's glory alone.

An excellent resource which can be used to train people in sharing their testimony can be found on the North American Mission Board website. You can download all of the materials to conduct a one hour or a one day workshop. Leader guides and student manuals are available in pdf format. The link for downloading this material follows:

http://www.namb.net/namb1pb2col.aspx?pageid=8589999486

Utilize every resource at your disposal to include the stories of people whose lives have been touched by the power of revival. Testimonies can be given live during regular services, pre-recorded as videos to be used during pre-service and post-service broadcasts, or as bulletin inserts, etc.

By including a broad selection of the church in these prayers and testimonies, additional interest is built toward revival. Use senior adults, married couples, and youth to share three minute testimonies. These testimonies should relate directly to what revival means to them. Some may have been converted during revivals or they may have made life changing decisions. Let the church see and hear how revival can make a difference.

Ushers T.E.A.M.

Seven minutes!

This is how long a church has to make a first impression. That impression does not begin after a person is seated in the auditorium. It begins the moment they turn off the highway and into your parking lot!

The ushers team is the front line welcoming force during the revival. They are the ones who make sure that those seven minutes are not wasted, because there will never be another opportunity to get those minutes back. Do-overs just are not allowed when it comes to church life. Since your revival will include many first time visitors it is important to have this team well prepared. These men and women should be given specific assignments outlining their duties.

All entrances to the building should have ushers stationed there at least thirty minutes before the services begin. Ushers should be prepared to direct visitors to the sanctuary, nursery, restrooms, etc.

It is a good idea to have husband and wife teams working together. Single parents (often mothers) can use an extra hand in getting children situated in the church. Remember, visitors will not know the closest route to the nursery. Ushers can build a high level of confidence in the minds of the visitors. Security is of high importance in today's churches. Well-trained ushers are an important part of overall security on the church grounds.

The parking lot should be well covered with ushers. Help visitors and church members from the moment they park their automobile. This is the best opportunity you will have to make a good first impression. Have umbrellas ready in case of inclement weather.

The Boy Scout motto is perfect for this team, *"Be Prepared!"*

Hospitality T.E.A.M.

The hospitality team will work as a liaison between the church and the evangelistic team. Their responsibilities will include the arrangement of meals for the evangelistic team. The hospitality team should be aware of any special dietary restrictions relative to the evangelist and others who will be participating in the meals. They will then make this information available to all who will be preparing the food.

Often traveling evangelists prefer dining at certain times of the day or not particularly eating three full meals each day. This team will determine all of this beforehand and plan accordingly.

In these times where most households consist of both husband and wife working outside of the home, it may be necessary to utilize restaurants for feeding the evangelistic team. Under such circumstances, gift cards to local restaurants can be provided by one or more of the church families. In this way, the church members can participate in providing meals in an indirect, but very effective fashion.

When the evangelistic team has travelled some distance they will often need local housing, transportation, laundering, or shopping to be done. This team can be helpful in arranging all of these needs for the evangelistic team.

As the hospitality team provides these services it allows the evangelist and his team more time to be adequately prepared for each day's services. Another advantage of this team's work benefits the church members also, since they can prepare ahead of time in their assistance. This gives everyone a greater opportunity to participate in all of the revival services.

Other T.E.A.M.'s

This section is for you to fill in at a later date as you discover unique and exciting ways of using the T.E.A.M. concept to release the power of revival in your church!

"Expectation has always been present in the church in the times of her greatest power. When she believed, she expected, and her Lord never disappointed her...Every great movement of God in history, every unusual advance in the church, every revival, has been preceded by a sense of keen anticipation. Expectation accompanied the operations of the Spirit always. His bestowals hardly surprised His people because they were gazing expectantly toward the risen Lord and looking confidently for His word to be fulfilled. His blessings accorded with their expectations.

— A.W. Tozer —

CONCLUSION

When the history books have completed the recording of the close of the twentieth century and the first decades of the twenty first, one must wonder if revival will have been a noteworthy event. As it has been said, "Time will tell!"

The church holds in her hands the tools of change for the world. Those tools may look different from one church to another. They may make diverse noises or they may be used with varied expertise. The tools used in preparing for revival, however, can make an impact upon society today.

The pastors, educational directors, youth directors, deacons, and others in leadership must come to grips with the reality of our need for revival. We need more than one more meeting. We need heaven-sent, Holy Spirit controlled, revival in our churches.

The laity of our churches are crying out for life and vitality from the pulpit to the pew. This work force of Christians is awaiting the call to service. We must stop telling them only **what** to do and begin informing them of the **how** and **when** also. We have no time to waste. We must redeem the time for the days are growing more and more evil as change rapidly comes upon us. (Ephesians 5:16).

It is our responsibility to equip the saints. God has already gifted us all. He can do no more. The church must take those gifted individuals and train them for the work—a work that will carry us through the twenty-first century and beyond.

Revival planning is part of that spiritual work. When we give them the tools of the trade, they will go to work. We must show them how and when to carry out the duties of the faith. The teams that will be developed will expand and soon the entire body of Christ will be engaged in the work of reaching the world for Christ

Some will doubtless claim that the plans of this book leave out the working of the Holy Spirit. On the contrary, these plans are based upon His sovereign work. No team should work under the presumption that the plan is an end of itself. Unless, the Spirit of the Lord goes before us in all of our planning, we will ultimately fail. (Psalm 127:1)

The principles given through these pages will need to be modified and customized for your individual work. That is one of the advantages of working for Christ. You never have to do anything the same way twice.

Use these guidelines for revival preparation as a starting point. Bathe your plans in prayer. Encourage full participation by all of those involved in your local ministry. Give ownership of the revival to the people and they will take part wholeheartedly.

Most of all, wait upon the Lord. Be diligent to prepare and then wait. God will pour out the blessing of revival in your life, in your church, and in your community. Until he comes again...

Let's Have a Revival!!!

ABOUT THE AUTHOR

R.E. Clark currently serves as the associational missionary for the Northwest Baptist Association in Bentonville, AR. He has ministered to these 69 churches, missions, and ministry points for the past 15 years. He earned his doctorate in ministry from the Southern Baptist Center in Jacksonville, Florida.

He brings to his writing style the experiences of over 33 years of ministry as a pastor and missions leader. In addition to nearly four decades of preaching and teaching, he has either led or participated in mission trips to Mexico, Nigeria, Haiti, Bosnia, Kenya, Brazil, China, Malaysia, and the Dominican Republic.

This book was first released in 1993 under the title, *The T.E.A.M. Concept of Revival Preparation.* The book was written directly as a result of the author's experiences as he created the first revival teams among the members of First Baptist Church in Livingston, LA.

His books now include two full year devotionals. *Glasses in the Grass: Devotions for My Friends* was released in 2012. His second devotional, *Life Is Not A Snapshot: It's A Mosaic* was released in 2013.

Book One of his *Life's Journey* series is now available under the title, God's Leading. Book Two, *God's Designing* will be released later this year. Two additional books in this series are being planned: *God's Speaking* and *God's Giving*. Look for them in the near future.

R.E. is married to his wife, Trudy. Both of them have suffered the loss of their first spouses. Trudy's first husband, a police officer, was killed in the line of duty. R.E.'s first wife died from the effects of Lou Gehrig's Disease. These tragic losses add to the author's writing style in a unique and genuine way. Their expanded family now consists of 8 children, 17 grandchildren, and 1 great-grandchild.

They reside in Centerton, AR.

You may contact the author through the following social media avenues:

Facebook: R.e. Clark
Twitter: GlassesnGrass
Blog: reclarkauthor.com
Email: reclark@reclarkauthor.com

ENDNOTES

1. Richard, Carwardine, *Transatlantic Revivalism*, page 116.

2. *Ibid.*, page 20.

3. Leonard Ravenhill, *Why Revival Tarries*, page 68.

4. John B. Boles, *The Great Revival 1787-1805*, page 40.

5. William G. McLoughlin, *Revivals, Awakenings, and Reform*, page 87.

6. Charles Hartshorn Maxson, *The Great Awakening in the Middle Colonies*, page 37.

7. Charles G. Finney, *How To Experience Revival*, pages 9-15.

8. Leonard Ravenhill, *Why Revival Tarries*, page 38.

9. Charles G. Finney, *How To Experience Revival*, page 74.

10. Richard Carwardine, *Transatlantic Revivalism*, page 140.

11. William G. McLoughlin, *Revivals, Awakenings, and Reform*, page 63.

12. William G. McLoughlin, *Revivals, Awakenings, and Reform*, pages 50-52

13. John B. Boles, *The Great Revival 1787-1805*, page 12.

14. *Ibid.*, page 30.

15. Jamie Buckingham, *Ministries Today*, Nov/Dec. 1991. pages 20-21.

16. Richard Carwardine, *Transatlantic Revivalism*, page 64.

17. William G. McLoughlin, *Revivals, Awakenings, and Reform*, page xiii.

18. *Ibid.*, page 36.

19. Charles Hartshorn Maxson, *The Great Awakening in the Middle Colonies*, page 16.

20. John B. Boles, *The Great Revival 1787-1805*, pages 30-31.

21. National and International Religion Report, "Fewer Than 10% of Americans", May 20, 1991, page 1.

22. Richard Carwardine, *Transatlantic Revivalism*, page 52.

23. *Ibid.*

24. William G. McLoughlin, *Revivals, Awakenings, and Reform*, page 66.

25. Richard Carwardine, *Transatlantic Revivalism*, page 45.

26. John B. Boles, *The Great Revival 1787-1805*, page 63.

27. Charles Hartshorn Maxson, *The Great Awakening in the Middle Colonies*, page 69.

28. *Ibid.*, pages 104-105.

29. *Ibid.*, page 91.

30. *Ibid.*, page 92.

31. *Ibid.*, pages 93-95.

32. William G. McLoughlin, *Revivals, Awakenings, and Reform,* page 31.

33. Richard Carwardine, *Transatlantic Revivalism*, pages 140-141.

34. Leonard Ravenhill, *Why Revival Tarries*, page 44.

35. Richard Carwardine, *Transatlantic Revivalism*, pages 54-55

36. Leonard Ravenhill, *Why Revival Tarries*, page 138.

37. *Ibid.*, Page 139.

38. John B. Boles, *The Great Revival*, page 61.

39. Leonard Ravenhill, *Why Revival Tarries*, page 131.

40. John B. Boles, *The Great Revival 1787-1805*, page 66.

41. Charles Hartshorn Maxson, *The Great Awakening in the Middle Colonies,* page 2.

42. *Ibid.*, page 150.

43. William G. McLoughlin, *Revivals, Awakenings, and Reform*, pages 60-62.

44. *Ibid.*, pages 63-66.

45. *Ibid.*, pages 45-45

46. *Ibid*, page 74.

47. John B. Boles, *The Great Revival 1787-1805*, page x.

48. *Ibid.*, pages 47-48.

49. William G. McLoughlin, *Revivals, Awakenings, and Reform*, pages 123-124.

50. *Ibid.*, page 125.

51. *Ibid.*, page 127.

52. C.E. Autrey, *Basic Evangelism*, page 107.

53. Bill V. Cathey, *A New Day in Church Revivals*, page 16.

54. L.F. Scarborough, *With Christ After the Lost*, pages 119-120.

55. C.E. Matthews, *The Southern Baptist Program of Evangelism*, page 40.

56. Bill V. Cathey, *A New Day in Church Revivals*, page 21.

57. Leonard Ravenhill, *Why Revival Tarries*, page 153.

58. Charles Lake, "Training Lay People—A Worthy Investment", *Decision Magazine*, October 1992, page 29.

59. Richard Carwardine, *Transatlantic Revivalism*; page 19.

60. *Ibid.*, page 89.

61. C.E. Matthews, *A Church Revival*, page 60.

SELECTED BIBLIOGRAPHY

Autrey, C.E., *Basic Evangelism*. Grand Rapids, Michigan: Zondervan Publishing House, 1959.

Barlow, George, *A Homiletic Commentary on the Epistles of St. Paul the Apostle to the Galatians, Ephesians. Philippians. Colossians and I. and II. Thessalonians.* in *The Preacher's Homiletic Commentary*, 32 vols.; New York: Funk and Wagnalls Company.

Boles, John B., *The Great Revival 1787-1805*. Lexington, Kentucky: The University Press of Kentucky, 1972.

Buckingham, Jamie, "Change with Society—or Die." *Ministries Today*, November/December 1991.

Cathey, Bill V., *A New Day in Church Revival*. Nashville, Tennessee: Broadman Press, 1984.

Carlin, Jr., David R., "Hoofbeats of Revival", *Commonweal*, 265-266, May 6, 1988.

Carwardine, Richard, *Transatlantic Revivalism*. Westport, Connecticut: Greenwood Press, 1978.

Editorial in *The Christian Century*, December 19-26, 1990. "Fewer Than 10% of Americans", *National and International Religion Report*, May 20, 1991.

Finney, Charles G., *How To Experience Revival*. Springdale, Pennsylvania: Whitaker House, 1984.

Hawkins, O.S. and Taylor, Jack, *When Revival Comes*. Nashville, Tennessee: Broadman Press, 1980.

Huston, Sterling W., *Crusade Evangelism and the Local Church*. Minneapolis, Minnesota: World Wide Publications, 1984.

Lake, Charles, "Training Lay People—A Worthy Investment", *Decision Magazine*. October 1992.

Matthews, C.E., *Church Revival*. Nashville, Tennessee: Broadman Press, 1955.

Matthews, C.E., *The Southern Baptist Program of Evangelism*. Nashville, Tennessee: Convention Press, 1956.

Maxson, Charles Hartshorn, *The Great Awakening in the Middle Colonies*. Gloucester, Massachusetts Smith, 1958.

McLoughlin, William G., *Revivals, Awakenings, and Reform*. Chicago: The University of Chicago Press, 1978.

Moody, D.L., *To The Work*. Chicago: PH. Revell Publishers, 1884.

O'Brien, Susan, "A Transatlantic Community of Saints: The Great Awakening and the First Evangelical Network, 1735-1755", *The American Historical Review*, 811-832, October 1986.

Pinnock, Clark H., *Three Keys to Spiritual Renewal*. Minneapolis, Minnesota: Bethany House Publishers, 1985.

Ravenhill, Leonard, *Why Revival Tarries*. Minneapolis, Minnesota: Bethany House Publishers, 1959.

Revival Training Seminar Notebook, Atlanta: Home Mission Board of the Southern Baptist Convention, 1981.

Scarborough, L.P., *With Christ After the Lost*. Nashville,Tennessee: Broadman Press, 1952.

Smith, Timothy L., *Revivalism and Social Reform*. New York: Abingdon Press, 1957.

Young, Doyle L., *New Life for Your Church*. Grand Rapids, Michigan: Baker Book House, 1989.

www.ingramcontent.com/pod-product-compliance
Lightning Source LLC
Chambersburg PA
CBHW060520030426
42337CB00015B/1951